How to Pass History
Basic Skills to Pass a College History Course

Andrés Tijerina

Kendall Hunt
publishing company

Cover image © Shutterstock, Inc.

www.kendallhunt.com
Send all inquiries to:
4050 Westmark Drive
Dubuque, IA 52004-1840

ISBN 978-0-7575-7848-9

Printed in the United States of America
10 9 8 7 6 5 4 3 2

Contents

Contents

Preface

This book was written after several years of teaching at small state universities and at the community college level, working with students who needed the basic skills to transfer and graduate from a major university. It is written to help the student who has passed all other courses, and now has to pass history at the last minute to obtain a degree. The basic skills and the style of writing are also directed at a student who may have failed history one or two semesters, and is still struggling to understand "What does the professor want?" I believe this student is willing to work harder than ever before if only he can be given assurance that he is using the best method finally to pass the course. Although the methods described in this book are designed for history courses, many of the skills are applicable to other disciplines. And although I wrote it specifically to give students a fail-safe way to pass a history course, my students have told me that it is more applicable in helping them achieve an A, rather than to simply pass.

Some of the chapters in this book suggest models which can be replicated for study, research, and writing in higher college or university levels. The chapter on writing a book report is generic, for example, but it may also suggest a model for the scholarly analysis of a history monograph by students in a lower-division undergraduate college history course. The methods, the didactic style, and the sometimes terse, imperative language is written with the specific objective of helping the student pass a test, write a quality product, or simply pass a college history course for three hours credit. This may seem to dismiss the more scholarly goals of advanced education, but those goals are implicit in the successful accomplishment of a college history course. My rationale is that if we professors can use tests in our quest for scholarship, then we can afford our students to focus primarily on passing those tests for the same lofty goal.

CHAPTER I

Reading a History Textbook

QUICK START

This chapter teaches you how to read a textbook and understand it well enough to pass a test on it. It includes a 1-page Quick Start instruction for those students who want to read the textbook immediately. The Quick Start is a comprehensive reading method that lets you quickly learn the facts that will be on a test. Some people like a Quick Start when they first open the box of a brand-new computer and do not wish to wade through the thick Owner's Manual. Likewise, in a history class, you can skip to the Quick Start first. But for a fuller explanation of how to really grasp the facts, you also have the option to read the following paragraphs in this chapter.

READING A TEXTBOOK

The purpose of this chapter is to help any student read the textbook well enough to pass the test. It's for students who want assurance that they are going to know the answers. They will learn the facts, but they want to know for sure. Some students may have doubts about their ability to pass a history test, so confidence is more important to them. They may have failed history in the past, and they want to make sure they don't fail again. I was like that as a college student.

When I took history my first semester in college, I was bored stiff. I slept through the lectures. And I barely passed the tests. That taught me two lessons. One, when I teach history, I want to teach only the part that is important for me to understand past human experience. And two, I wanted facts that would help me pass the test. Too often, I was left wondering what the professor wanted on the test. Some people want the straight facts. They don't want to wonder "Is this what the professor wants?" They want to know "Do I have to know this or not?" They want to know what they have to know to pass the test.

A lot of people really don't mind reading long history chapters as long as they know that it will pay off with a good grade. My belief is that people are perfectly willing to read and to work hard. Indeed, they actually want to work hard. They just want to know that it's going to pay off in a good grade. This chapter teaches the student how to find the facts that count—the facts that will be on the test.

LOSE THE BAD HABITS

One of the first issues that has to be corrected is to unlearn the old way of reading. If a student failed a history course, or if they are now struggling in history class, they probably have bad habits. One bad habit from high school is to party every Friday night. It's fun, but it's more than fun. It's a habit. And it's a very bad habit for a college student who has a big test on Monday. Some college students never shake that habit, and they find themselves going home before the end of their first semester in college. Another bad habit is to get up from reading after only 30 minutes to take a break or to call the boyfriend. They simply cannot sit for one or two hours without jumping up to get away from the book.

Skimming over the detailed facts in a paragraph is another bad habit students bring from high school. Skimming through the chapter to read just the chapter title and subheadings is like licking the wrapper on a hamburger. It smells good, but there's no protein in it. Skimming is fast, but the student never reads the answers to the test questions. The only good use in skimming a history book is when they later come back and read it intensively as well. Skimming is good for orientation to the chapter, but it is not reading and the student never gets to read the test questions in the chapter. This chapter will talk about how to get rid of those bad habits. Quickly. Effectively.

FORGET THE EXCUSES

Another issue that has to be addressed is the excuse of slow readers and bored readers. Some people feel that they are at a disadvantage because they read slowly. Others may feel confident because they have always loved history. Reading slowly or loving history doesn't really matter because they don't affect test performance. A slow reader who can learn the facts can still pass the test as well as a fast reader. Slow readers may take longer to read the chapter, but they may understand it better. What's important is to learn the facts. It's not important how fast you read, but what you intake. I have a PhD and I read very, very slowly, even sometimes moving my lips to pronounce the words one at a time. But when I finish a sentence, I remember the important point in that sentence. And I'd remember it two weeks later for a test.

You don't have to love reading history to do well. In fact, you can hate history and still pass a test. The important issue is "Do you know the answers?" You can know answers that you don't like just as well as you can know answers that you love. In a history textbook, a student reads specifically to identify the important facts, whether they are fun facts or boring facts. An example of this specific reading is in a printed warranty that comes with a new product. You never heard anybody say that their product warranty was fascinating reading, but they read it anyway. Even if it was boring. Why did they read it? Because it's important.

FIND THE IMPORTANT FACTS

When a customer buys a product—for $500, he makes sure to get the printed warranty. If the product breaks, the first thing he does is read the warranty specifically until he finds the clause that says "90 days plus parts and labor." He takes the product back—and waves the warranty in the clerk's face, and demands the parts and repairs. He is confident because he specifically read the important facts in the warranty. Was it fascinating reading? No. Did he just love reading the warranty? Absolutely not. Did it give him goose bumps? No. The customer read the warranty specifically for the important facts, and he waded through all the fine print and the pages of legal disclaimers until he found the clause that he knew was important—"90 days plus parts and labor." He is smart enough to read through the boring small print in the warranty, and he certainly can read a boring history textbook. It does not matter if history is boring or fascinating. It only matters that the reader is committed to finding the important facts. A history book has facts.

A history textbook is different in many ways from other books. It is written to teach facts. Facts. Not feelings. Not formulas. Not rhythm or rhyme. It has no poetry. Just facts. For that reason, you cannot read the history textbook using the same methods as other college courses. Learn to read the history textbook to look for the facts. Make a note of the facts, and write notes about the facts. Learn the facts, and remember them for the test. The test is on the facts. Only facts.

In other words, the history professor is going to ask the students for facts, not how the chapter made them feel. In English literature, as an example, the class may read poetry or drama, and their professor may ask them about love and emotions expressed in the poetry. A history professor, on the other hand, will not ask the class if the history book made them feel forlorn or inspired. The history professor asks the class only to identify specific facts in the chapter. Those are the facts that will be on the test. In history class then, you should learn to read the textbook specifically to identify the facts.

CRITICAL ANALYSIS

As you learn to read the facts in a history textbook, you develop the habit of writing down those facts to remember them for the test. But the history test does not ask for simple facts like dates and names.

It will not ask for a simple name like "Who sailed the ocean blue in fourteen hundred ninety-two?" or for a simple date like "Which year did Columbus sail to the New World?" In fact, most college students actually resent being asked to know simple facts that have no significance. They feel as if they wasted their time to learn simple dates. They want to know that the facts they are studying are critical to understanding their own world and their own lives. That's critical analysis.

Critical analysis is reading to identify the importance of facts, or the important concepts—being critical of the history book. Not being cynical, but checking that the story is sensible and that the book gives you evidence that it is true and logical.

Columbus sailed in 1492. OK. So what? So nothing. Nobody cared about what year it was except his poor mother back at home.

Unless you consider the fact that his sailors had diseases like measles and smallpox. That when they landed and greeted the natives in America, they unwittingly transmitted the world's most deadly disease to a million people who had absolutely no immunity to those diseases. That within about 60 years, millions and millions of the American natives had died and left few families, soldiers, or even government to fight off the European encroachment.

So what's important? The date 1492, or the catastrophic death of millions of human beings? The important concept is that millions of natives died on contact with the Europeans.

The history textbook teaches dates, names, and events, but a student has to be able to learn that the important concept is the result of those events in history. The student has to analyze or to identify the important concept in those facts.

The simple date is 1492. The simple name is Christopher Columbus. But the important concept is that the landing of Europeans in America brought catastrophic change to the native civilizations. That's critical analysis. Critical analysis is analyzing the facts to find the important concept.

The history textbook teaches the simple facts and the critical analysis as well. It's up to you to learn to distinguish between simple facts and important concept. Luckily for you, most textbooks are written in a format that helps to identify these concepts. The paragraph might say, for example, "The landing of Columbus in 1492 was dramatic, but it is most significant for the catastrophic changes it brought to the native populations." You can read all the facts, but you learn to identify the important ones. You learn to analyze critically. The history test will then ask you to identify the important concept. Sample test questions are discussed in a later chapter, but here's one just to demonstrate critical analysis:

When Columbus landed in the New World, Native Americans were most impacted by:

A) the clothing of the Europeans.   *B) the names of Columbus' three ships.*

C) the European calendar.   *D) European diseases.*

Answer D correctly identifies the important fact. The other choices may be correct and true, but they are not the most important concept.

FINDING THE IMPORTANT CONCEPT

In this discussion, two things should be clear about reading a history textbook: One is that you must read the text intensively, word by word, not simply skim over the paragraphs to get general impressions. And the other is that you must read the textbook actively to search for the answers to the test questions. That is it. Those are the two basic functions in reading a textbook.

Read it intensively.

Identify the concepts that will be on the test.

Each paragraph has an important concept, and you must find it to be ready for the test. In fact, you may well imagine that while you are reading one paragraph in the textbook, the professor is reading the same paragraph at the same time. The difference is that the professor is composing the test while he reads that paragraph. He's asking "What test question can I write from this paragraph?" The professor reads it in the same way that you do and the professor identifies the same important concept as you for the same paragraph. Each one writes a note. You write a note on the important concept. And the professor writes a test question for that important concept.

Is it possible for you to find the same important concept that the professor finds in a paragraph? Yes. You are as smart as the professor. Any student can probably read as fast as the professor, if not faster. And any student can interpret conclusions as well as the professor.

There are some differences in the student and the professor, of course. Any student hasn't read 2,000 books on the subject. A student hasn't written several books on the subject, and the student doesn't know nine other facts about that important concept in the paragraph. But the paragraph has only one important concept, not ten. The other nine concepts that the professor knows are not in this paragraph. This paragraph has only one important concept, and any student can grasp it as well as the professor can. In fact, in ten paragraphs, the student could probably grasp nine out of ten of the same concepts as the professor from reading the same ten paragraphs. That is because the textbook is usually written to give only one important concept for each paragraph, and it is written to make the important concept identifiable to anyone who can read tenth-grade English. Anyone—the student or the professor.

The one definite advantage the professor has over a tenth grader in reading a textbook is that the professor has developed the discipline to sit down and read the paragraph intensively without getting up to call the boyfriend or play a computer game. But for a student who can develop the skill to sit down and intensively identify the important concept for each paragraph in the chapter, then the textbook is a level playing field for anyone. That is what this chapter is all about. The objective was stated earlier above: The purpose of this chapter is to help any student read the textbook well enough to pass the test.

THE STUDY ROOM

So how do you sit down and read intensively? The foundation for reading intensively is to read in a controlled environment—a quiet place to study. This means that you must deliberately set aside a period of time to read with no noise or physical distractions. It also means that you should have resources and reading habits that enhance the comprehension of the reading material. Serious readers know that they need these advantages. For students who have long-established poor reading habits, on the other hand, the need for a good reading environment may seem trivial or optional. In fact, these points seem difficult to justify because most people are accustomed to ordinary reading every day with none of these advantages. A busy professional may be accustomed to reading the newspaper while rushing through breakfast in a fast food restaurant. A customer opens the box of a new product and quickly reads through the assembly instructions before trying it for the first time, and it works. A youthful reader reads a popular novel from start to finish in a few days, and comprehends it well enough to discuss the plot with friends online. Or a high school student skims through a chapter in a history textbook and answers a few subjective questions to pass the high school history test. All of these examples serve to explain why many college freshmen are shocked when they fail their first college history test. They realize that the test questions are much more specific than they expected. But instead of admitting that they couldn't identify the important concepts because they used a superficial reading method, they blame it on the professor. Or, they complain that the test questions are unfairly specific. That the test is unfair. In reality, the ordinary reading method is not adequate for the intensive reading level required in a college history course.

A college history student has to identify and retain the important concepts to pass a test. And in reality, even a casual reader knows this. That's why, when somebody finds a sensational fact in a magazine, they turn down the television and tell everyone to be quiet while they read the sensational news. Why tell everybody to be quiet? Because they know instinctively that they must have silence in order to effectively grasp the important concept. And that's all you have to do in order to grasp the important concept in a history textbook.

Sit down. Shut up. And read quietly. For hours.

THE READING SET UP

Long before a college student sits down to read a history textbook, he has to set aside the time to read. This is time management. It means the student has to look at his week's schedule and mark the time and days he will give himself the time to do his reading. One college student may work part-time at the grocery store weekend mornings. That means he has to read on those afternoons and on Monday through Wednesday mornings. Another student may be taking 15 hours of college courses and spend hours in the laboratory every night. That means he has to do his history reading in the mornings or late at night. Time management means the student actively marks on a weekly schedule the days and hours he will set aside for history textbook reading. And it means he will give up some other activity. The problem is that the other activities are important and the student would have to make a sacrifice to give them up just for reading history. That is time management. Time management is giving up something important. It is making a sacrifice to read a history textbook instead. It has to be a sacrifice; otherwise, the student will never have the time to read history. If you don't give up something important, you'll never read your history book because everything is important. The question is not "When do you have free time?" You never have free time. The question is "Do you want to give up that important house chore or do you want to give up your college diploma? Which is it?"

Give up the beer with the pals, and read from 8 to 10 PM at the library. And don't plan to read for only 30 minutes. That's not going to get you through a chapter in a history textbook. History professors don't write textbooks with single-liners and 30-second sound bites. They write concepts constructed from a complex series of facts. You are capable of easily grasping those concepts, but the serious student will need at least one hour of intensive reading. At least one hour. After sitting down to read a history textbook, you don't get up to adjust the light. You don't get up to answer the phone, or to use the rest room. You make a serious time commitment. You can take a break every one hour, but you don't take a history textbook to the bathroom. Do that with a Hollywood magazine. For a history textbook, you need to make a realistic commitment of time like three to four hours at a sitting with no disturbance. Did you say you don't have four hours to read history? How long do you flip hamburgers at the part-time job? Four hours? Working for someone else? Well give yourself the same four hours for reading because these four hours will change your life. Four hours flipping hamburgers is four hours of life lost. Reading a book builds skill. And it's not for someone else. The comprehension of important concepts in a history textbook require a time commitment throughout the work week, just like a part-time job.

To use your dedicated time efficiently, you must sit down in a controlled environment. In order to think seriously about the facts in the textbook, you must have silence and no distractions. This means you can't read history while riding the bus. You can't sit in front of the television or in a crowd of friends and read history. You sit in a room with four walls around you. Not at the window, not in the hall. Omar Kayyám sat underneath a bough with a loaf of bread and a jug of wine. But Omar was reading love poems, not a history textbook for a test next Monday. No jug of wine, no trees. Just four walls. It is no accident that graduate students sit in a library at a small desk called a graduate carrel. A graduate carrel is the little table you see in the corner of the library. It typically has three walls—two sidewalls and one in front. The graduate student sticks his head in and glues himself to the reading. All you see is the back of his head. For hours. Why do they call it a graduate carrel? Because it's designed for people who are getting a PhD. They are doing serious graduate-level reading. Do you want to do serious reading? You can sit in the kitchen while Mom cooks dinner if you want. Or you can commit three hours to go to the library and sit in a graduate carrel and really grasp the facts for the history test. Read in controlled environment designed for college students who are going to pass and graduate.

USE A DICTIONARY

Now that you are sitting in a quiet place for three hours of serious reading, you need to use all the resources available to get a full understanding of the reading material. One of the basics of reading a history textbook is a dictionary. A dictionary is as integral to the history student as a calculator is to the math student. Many undergraduates scoff at the idea of using a dictionary. That's because maybe they never read a book that uses so many complex terms as a college history textbook. Or maybe it's because they haven't failed their college history course yet. When I ask students why they failed their freshman history course, very often they reply that they simply did not understand the readings. And very often it comes down to one word that they did not know in the sentence.

One word. In a history textbook, one word can be critical. It may be the one word that completes the multiple-choice question on the test. One word in a sentence is like the proverbial nail in the old medieval rhyme:

For want of a nail, a shoe was lost
For want of a shoe, a horse was lost
For want of a horse, a rider was lost
For want of a rider, a battle was lost
For want of a battle, a kingdom was lost

In other words, one minor mistake can have major consequences.

In history class, the rhyme goes like this:

For want of a word, a sentence was lost
For want of a sentence, a paragraph was lost
For want of a paragraph, an important concept was lost
For want of an important concept, a test question was lost
For want of a test question, a test was lost
For want of a test, a history course was lost.

Not a semester goes by that at least one student doesn't come by begging for one point to bring his average up. "But I need this course to graduate." Or "I need this grade to bring up my GPA to keep my scholarship." One two-point question is important.

One word missed in a sentence may not sound like much until you see it later in a multiple-choice question. Then it can change the multiple-choice answer. If you don't know the meaning of the word, you cannot know the multiple-choice answer. You can look it up if the professor lets you look it up in the dictionary during a test. But a test is the wrong time to be looking up words in the dictionary.

The reality is that a history textbook doesn't have a big word. It's nothing but big words, and complex terms. The whole book, front to back. History is written in standard modern professional American English. It's written with the words used by professionals in any field. Chemists, mathematicians, doctors, and computer technicians all have their unique technical terms, but in memos and directives, everybody has to use standard professional English. Standard professional English is what you'll be using when you become a manager in your own field, whether you are a nurse or an engineer. And all the best engineers become managers. All the best nurses become managers at some point in their career. And they'll be using the words learned in a history textbook. No technical terms, no equations, no medical terms; just standard professional American English. If you can learn the words used in a history textbook, you'll build the vocabulary you will use for the rest of your professional career, regardless of your field. But don't try to learn a word during a test. Learn it while you're reading your textbook. And for that, you need a dictionary.

The proper dictionary for reading a history textbook is the collegiate dictionary. It should be a dictionary of standard American English, not Oxford British English and not an informal dictionary. It should provide the full definitions and good examples of usage. You can't build a vocabulary using a simple pocketbook dictionary or an online dictionary with simple one-line definitions. Buy a collegiate dictionary. It may cost a few dollars, but it easily justifies the cost. One of the common objections to buying a dictionary is that it is just one more book to buy, but a good collegiate dictionary costs less than any other book you will buy. A dictionary costs much less than a math calculator, and it lasts decades longer. Indeed, it is one book that almost every college graduate keeps in his professional library after graduation.

The correct way to use a dictionary is to lay it on your desk beside the textbook while reading. As you are reading the paragraph, each time you arrive at a word that you don't know, stop. Put the textbook down. Take up the dictionary and look up the word. Read the definition and then return to the textbook. Apply the new word meaning to understand the important concept of the paragraph. At the same time, you will be practicing your first correct use of the word. Not only will it help you understand the important concept, but you internalize the word. Look it up one time, and it will be yours forever.

Another objection that undergraduate students have to using a dictionary is that it interrupts the reading. And that looking up a word can double the reading time. That is true. The dictionary is a major time commitment a student has to make, but it easily justifies itself. You will find that the textbook often uses the same words throughout the chapter. After you internalize a word the first time, you will never have to look it up again, and as you build a vocabulary, it accelerates reading the rest of the textbook. These are the words that you will see on the test questions, and they are the words you will use when you write a memo to your employees after college. In fact, vocabulary is one of the most obvious differences between the boss and the employees. He has a professional vocabulary that he built reading the textbook. And not after he gets his first job. That's the worse time to try to catch up building a professional vocabulary. Your competition is building their vocabulary right now in college. And you need to have your vocabulary ready to hit the ground running when you get your first job. This is the time to do it, and this is the best way to do it. The first time you run into a word you don't know:

Stop reading.

Take up the dictionary.

Look up the word.

Apply the word in the paragraph.

Read on until you get to the next new word.

Stop reading, and so on.

GRAPHICS, CHARTS, AND MAPS

Another difference in reading a history textbook is that in history, you do have to study the illustrations, maps, charts, graphs, and so on. The graphics reinforce the text. Ordinary reading is simple enough that the reader can easily grasp the meaning and remember the main fact. If, for example, a reader is reading poems in a literature book, he hardly stops to look at a picture of Shakespeare's old Globe Theater in the book. But reading in a history textbook, the reader needs to stop and study the graphics. A history textbook has a great volume of facts, and the meaning must be analyzed for the important concept. A reader can be overwhelmed if he or she tries to read a history textbook the same as a novel or a simple narrative. In history, the reader must build skills to analyze and remember all the facts. Students commonly complain that the history textbook is boring, confusing, and has too many names and dates. That's true—if a student is trying to read it like a story book. That's like trying to do brain surgery with a spoon. A surgeon had to learn skills to be a brain surgeon, and he had to learn to use specialized tools. Likewise, if you want to be a professional, you also need to learn new reading skills and to use your new specialized reading tools. One of those skills is to use graphics to reinforce your reading comprehension.

A map in a history textbook serves two purposes. It shows graphically the location of events. A map can explain why a general was cornered in a battlefield and forced to surrender. The other main purpose of the map is to help imprint the message in the reader's brain. The reader already read the message as text. Now, he reinforces the text with a visual image. He has two mental imprints for the same message: one in text and one in graphics. Both reinforce the lesson.

The history student needs both mental imprints to remember that lesson, because two weeks later, he's going to be confused on the test. He'll be nervous on the test, and wonder if he knows the correct answer. But if he read the text and studied the map as well, he'll remember the lesson because it was firmly imprinted in his brain. In the past, you did not need the double imprint for a simple fact. But you are no longer a high school student reading ordinary text. Now, you are reading a complex paragraph, and you must remember the facts for a test two weeks later. For that, you need all the advantages you can get. Studying the map is an important skill that gives the college student that extra advantage.

Other graphic resources include charts, archival documents, and illustrations. They all serve to graphically reinforce the textual message. And unlike other college disciplines, a history test sometimes has multiple-choice questions about the graphic. One typical question on a graphic, for example, is on a chart that shows population growth in a period of years. The question might ask in which year the population declined. That answer came only from the chart. In that way, the graphic not only reinforced the correct answer. It was the correct answer. Common test questions also ask details on maps like where certain crops are grown, like cotton in the south. Develop the skill of reading, studying, and taking notes on graphics to reinforce the important concepts in the history textbook.

COACH'S CORNER

Use a dictionary?   **Study in the library?**

Read every word?   **Sit for three hours straight?**

That's a bunch of picky little details, isn't it?

YES. Come to think of it, only two of my students ever really cared about these picky little details:

  1. The guy who wanted an A.

  2. The guy who flunked history and wanted to know why he flunked.

They're not pick little details. THEY'RE SKILLS. Use them.

STEPS TO READING A HISTORY TEXTBOOK

Orientation: Skim the Chapter

That's right. Before you read a chapter for details, skim through it. Just like they taught in high school. It should take about 5 or 10 minutes to skim the entire chapter. Read the chapter title. Read the introductory paragraph just to get an idea about the subject of the chapter. Read the title of the first subsection, then read the title of the second subsection, and proceed to read the other subsection titles to the end of the chapter. Stop to look at the graphics. Read any bordered boxes on the page to get an idea of the lessons they are teaching. Skim through the whole chapter, trying to guess the topic or the lesson for each paragraph or subsection. For example, a subsection entitled "Eli Whitney's New Cotton Gin" is probably about Eli Whitney inventing the cotton gin. That's how simple it is.

Now, here's a question: Do you think you are correctly guessing the paragraph topics?

Answer: Yes.

You can correctly guess the topic of a subsection by simply reading the title in most cases. You do have to think about it, but you can get pretty close. Guess the topic of each paragraph quickly for the entire chapter.

Learning Objectives

Don't just guess the topics in the chapter. Guess the lesson for each paragraph and subsection—the important concept. As you guess the topic of a paragraph, guess the important concept you think the paragraph will teach you. This is called questioning. That is, you question the paragraph. As an example, you say "I think this paragraph is teaching me that the cotton gin increased cotton production." Think of a question for each paragraph or subsection. This is a critical step in reading a textbook. This is the scientific method developed by philosophers hundreds of years ago that allowed humanity to advance beyond simple observation. Aristotle began to not only observe life and existence. He questioned it. And he began to set a hypothesis of his observation. In other words, he not only observed ants. He hypothesized that ants worked together as social animals. A scientist first observes a process, and then he sets a hypothesis to explain how it works or why. When you question a paragraph, you are setting a hypothesis about the important concept. That advances you beyond simple reading. In effect, you are setting a learning objective for yourself. You are determining to go back and learn that answer.

Setting a hypothesis or learning objective is important because it stimulates your brain to search for the answer. You know very well that just guessing at the important concept will be wrong half the time. You haven't even read the paragraph yet. You just read the title and looked at the words. But you made an educated guess, and by wondering about the important concept, you opened your mind to inquiry. You gave your mind an objective to learn the true important concept. Your mind will not stop wondering about that concept until it goes back to verify the true important concept. Your mind actually wants to read the paragraph now. That comes next.

Read to Understand

Now that you have set a learning objective for every paragraph or subsection in the chapter, go back and read them one at a time to verify your hypothesis for each one. This time, you read the paragraph intensively, in a serious search for the important concept. Your hypothesis may prove to be correct, or it may be completely wrong. If your hypothesis is correct, you will be rewarded with a sense of satisfaction that you correctly identified the important concept. If your hypothesis is not correct, you will immediately recognize the wrong hypothesis because you have now read the correct important concept. Either way, you identified the correct important concept for the paragraph, and you can be confident that you know it. That is the purpose of setting a learning objective. It confirms the important concept.

By the way, if you do not want to skim and set learning objectives before reading a textbook chapter, you don't have to. You can read it like an average reader, and get average grades. Or less than average.

Sample Reading Exercise

When you read a paragraph in a history textbook, pay attention to what you are reading. Do not just read the words and hope that they will make sense later. Do the following exercise to measure your own reading style. Follow the instructions step by step. To begin, read the following sample sentence:

> The most victorious European lords became monarchs by the fifteenth century and erected the institutions of modern government, including various bureaucratic mechanisms for collecting taxes, enacting legislation, and enforcing laws over large domains. These new monarchs were thereby able to perpetuate their nation-states.[1]

Stop.

Cover up the sample sentence above, using your pen or your hand. Don't peek. For a good indication of your reading style, discipline yourself to cover it so you can't read it. Now, with the sample sentence covered completely, recite aloud in your own words the meaning of the sentence you just read. Do not go back to read it. Take a pen and write your answers to complete the following sentences in the lines below:

The major actors in this sentence were ___European lords___

_____.

The kings erected governments with ___taxes, rules,___

_____.

They did this in the ___15th___ century.

It took place on the continent of ___Europe___.

The kings were thereby able to ___preserve nation states___

_____.

Did you know the answers to each of the questions above? How many answers did you know?

Now, uncover the sample sentence and read the complete sentence one more time. After carefully reading the sentence the second time, answer the following questions as shown below:

Who were the major actors in the sentence?
The major actors in this sentence were lords who became kings.

What did they do?
The kings erected governments with taxes, legislation, and law enforcement.

When did they do it?
In the mid-fifteenth century.

Where did the action take place?
On the continent of Europe.

Why did they do it?
With these institutions, the kings were able to perpetuate their new nation-states.

Evaluate Your Reading Style

Now that you see the facts in the sample sentence, evaluate your own reading effectiveness. Did you know all of the answers? Half of them? None of them?

Compare your first sample sentence reading to the second time you read it. Most students cannot recite a single fact from the sample sentence the first time they read it. Not one fact. In a classroom of 36 college students, typically not one single student can recite even the main topic in the sentence. Even the student who volunteered to read the sentence aloud in class is not able to recite a single fact from his own sample reading.

How can 36 students read a sentence together and not a single one of them be able to identify even the main topic? It happens in my class every semester. Here's a better question: Why did you know all the answers on the second reading?

The reason you knew the answers on the second reading is that you knew you would be asked to recite the facts. And the reason you did not know the answers the first time you read it is that you were not paying attention to the facts you were reading in the sentence. That is a bad habit that most students are not aware they have until they do this sample reading exercise. If you knew all the facts the first time you read the sentence (without looking), your reading will give you an advantage on research, writing, and other areas you may not do as well.

The first lesson to learn from this sample reading is that the next time you read a sentence in history, pay attention to what you are reading. Read every single sentence. And at the end of every sentence, stop to check yourself that you really know what you just read—as if you were going to be asked to recite it in class. The second lesson is don't ever allow yourself to sleepwalk through a sentence again. From now on, when you read in a history textbook, read to understand.

This is also a good time to remember that the sample sentence had at least one word that may not be familiar to many undergraduate students. Do you know the accurate meaning of the word *perpetuate*? Do you know it well enough to trust it to answer a two-point multiple-choice question? Do you know the accurate meaning of the word *feudal*? Now is when you make your commitment to looking up a word that will be on the test. If *feudal* is in the textbook paragraph, that means it has a good chance of being one of the choices in a multiple-choice question on the test. Stop. Look it up. Go back to the reading and apply your new vocabulary word. Now that you are paying attention, start reading a history textbook.

Underline and Highlight

While reading through a paragraph, it is common for students to underline words with a pen or to highlight them with a colored highlighter. This is good only if it is done correctly. The purpose of highlighting in a paragraph is to come back later to quickly review the paragraph before a test. The highlighted words focus the eyes quickly to the key words or phrases without having to re-read the whole paragraph a second time. This is why it is important to highlight only a few words in a paragraph—no more than three or four words, or perhaps only a short phrase. Highlight only the name of a general, the date of an invention, or a major court case. Later, a quick look at the paragraph quickly reminds you of those details.

However, if the entire paragraph is highlighted, then you have to read the entire paragraph later when you come back to review it. You had to read the paragraph twice. The obvious choice is to skip the review rather than read the entire paragraph a second time. That defeats the purpose of highlighting. Highlight only one word in a sentence. Highlight only three or four words in a paragraph, or a short phrase.

Synthesize and Internalize

Now that you are settled into a quiet reading time and space, and you are paying attention to your reading, it is time to learn the most important skill in reading a history textbook. That skill is identifying the important concept. Each paragraph or subsection has a main point that the textbook author has put there for the reader. Your job is to find that concept and understand it. These are the two college-level skills you must learn to perform in each paragraph. Identify. Synthesize.

To identify the important concept in a paragraph, you first read the entire paragraph as described above. That is, you pay attention to the meaning and facts, reading each sentence one at a time. You use a dictionary to assure that you understand the word meanings. You highlight a few key words. After you finish reading a paragraph, you synthesize the paragraph.

To synthesize the paragraph, you think back to the learning objective you previously set for it. Earlier, when you skimmed the paragraph, you read only the subsection title and guessed your hypothesis for the subject. For example, earlier you read the subsection title "River

Transport," you saw a graphic of a steamboat, and you noticed Robert Fulton's name. You might have guessed that the paragraph was about Robert Fulton and the steamboat. And you might have hypothesized that this paragraph would teach you how Robert Fulton came to invent the steamboat. Now you actually read the paragraph.

After reading the entire paragraph, sentence by sentence, stop reading.

Do not read on to the next paragraph.

Look away from the textbook.

Review in your mind all the names, dates, events, and action of the paragraph. In a paragraph, for example, you may have read or highlighted several facts like the ones listed below:

James Watts first patented the steam engine

Mississippi River and Ohio River transportation

steamboat transportation

American agricultural production in the old Northwest

Robert Fulton, inventor

the *Clermont* steamboat model

Clermont invented in 1807

lower transportation costs and higher profits

Now, as you are thinking about these, try to draw a conclusion or a lesson in this paragraph. The paragraph has many facts, and it teaches more than one lesson. Your task is to decide for yourself which is the most important lesson. That one is the important concept. Your skill is to go step by step to identify it. This is called synthesizing. Next are the simple steps to synthesizing a paragraph.

Synthesizing

First, using your own words, make a list of two or three of the lessons, events, or actions that the paragraph is describing. For example, you may list these three:

1. James Watts first patented his invention of a steam engine.

2. American farmers greatly increased their crop production in the Ohio River Valley.

3. Robert Fulton invented a compact river steamboat called the *Clermont* that carried more cargo.

Second, select the one lesson that is the most important. You may choose to combine parts of them into one. For example, you might say "This paragraph says that to help American farmers take their bulk crops to market, Robert Fulton invented the *Clermont* to carry more cargo for greater profits."

Third, shorten your sentence into a few key words, for example, "Robert Fulton's *Clermont* made steamboat transportation profitable." Summarizing the facts to form a single conclusion is called synthesizing. You not only read the paragraph, you synthesized it. The difference is that you did not simply accept the simple facts. You combined the facts that you read with your own logic to form the conclusion. This is the synthesis. The facts you read are the thesis. Your logic is the hypothesis, and the combination is the synthesis. In synthesizing the paragraph, you have successfully identified the important concept. The synthesis is the important concept. But most important, it is the question your professor will ask as a multiple-choice on the test.

To prepare for the test, simply invert your important concept into a question, for example, "*Who made steamboat transportation profitable?*" Answer: Robert Fulton.

The introduction of this chapter indicated that it would teach the student how to find the facts that count—the facts that will be on the test. It also stated that an answer identified through the synthesizing process described above would have a very high chance of being the same important concept that the professor would have on the test. This method offers assurance that any undergraduate can use the same controlled intensive reading used by graduate students. It also offers to help a student to identify the same question in a paragraph that the textbook author and your professor would likely see in that paragraph. This method requires much more controlled reading than many undergraduate students may be accustomed to using. It probably requires much more time commitment as well. But as much work as it requires to this point, it still is not enough to pass the test. That is because synthesizing only identifies the important concept for the student. Identifying the important concept does not assure that the student will remember it on the test. For that, the student must internalize the important concept. Not memorize it. Internalize it.

Internalizing

Internalizing means learning. It means also that a person accepts a concept as part of their thinking process. They synthesized their own logic and life experiences to analyze the facts in the textbook, so now they're ready to commit it to memory. This is the follow-up process to identifying the important concept. But internalizing is not simply memorizing data or facts without analyzing them like a high school student memorizing the presidents. It is a step-by-step method to help the student remember the answers for the test. It starts by writing keynotes in the margin to identify the important concepts for each paragraph in a chapter. Next, the reader goes back to recall those marginal keynotes. And the last step is to do an exercise drill with those keynotes. The three steps are keynote, recall, and drill.

Notes

After a reader has massaged a paragraph to identify its important concept, he must now write his own brief note for that paragraph. The note should help him quickly recall the important concept without having to go back and re-read the paragraph. The note should be no more than three keywords, not necessarily flowing as a sentence. For example, to write a note about Robert Fulton's steamboat, the reader may simply write in the margin next to the paragraph:

Fulton *Clermont* profitable

Students are tempted to write longer notes for the paragraphs, but long notes are not necessary. Longer notes require more reading when the student comes back to re-read them later. Notes only need to trigger a word association. That is, they are only keywords that the student mentally associates to the concept that he synthesized earlier. Each keyword represents a thought that the student had when he was synthesizing the paragraph. By re-reading the note, the student can recall a great number of facts from his reading of the paragraph because he read each sentence and carefully synthesized all of the lessons in the paragraph. You can remember much more than just the important concept. As an example, read the three keywords above. Ask yourself this question, "What was the *Clermont*?" You knew it was a steamboat. Ask yourself another question, "Who were the people who most profited from this steamboat?" Ask another question, "What kind of cargo became more profitable?" You probably knew it was farmers who profited with a cargo of bulk crops. Indeed, most students can recall even more details. They can recall specific facts like the date 1807, the names of the Mississippi and Ohio rivers, and James Watts' first steam engine patent.

By using keywords, a typical student can recall not only the important concept. A student can recall many, many other details—even more details than they intended. That is because a person is capable of recalling details through the word association process. Internalization is highly effective in using keywords to recall the important concept of a paragraph.

There are two curious characteristics about recalling facts in a history textbook. One is how many facts can be recalled when a reader uses notes. The other is how few facts can be recalled when a reader does not use notes. In fact, a reader can easily be overwhelmed reading all the facts in a history textbook chapter. Unless he takes it step by step to synthesize each paragraph, stop, and write a note for each paragraph. When he does, the reader can control not only the great volume of facts, but he can synthesize and internalize them. The difference between being overwhelmed and being in control is simply to use a step-by-step method. Stop. Synthesize. Note. And remember, the note is a simple note of three keywords. Now, after reading the chapter, the reader should have a note in the margin beside each paragraph or subsection in the chapter.

Re-Read and Recall

By now, the reader has spent several hours reading the textbook chapter. He has taken extra time to use learn dictionary meanings for any difficult words, used the graphics, and identified a important concept for every paragraph or subsection. And he now has written a keyword note beside every single one. Now it is time to go back to the start of the chapter, and read it all over again—this time reading only the marginal notes. He does not re-read the text in the paragraph, only the note in the margin. As he reads the note in the margin, he strives to recall the important concept for that paragraph. He might glance at the paragraph text, but only to check his highlighted words for extra details. His main focus is to recall the important concept. It is the test question.

After reading the keywords in the marginal note, recalling the important concept, the reader then advances on to the marginal note for the next paragraph. He reads that note, recalls the concept, and moves on in this process through the entire paragraph. As stated above, it is curious that a serious reader can recall a great percentage of the concepts and facts. But if along the way, the reader is unable to recall the important concept clearly, then he stops to check his highlighted words, and even parts of the paragraph text to assist in triggering the keyword associations. Either way, the reader re-reads the entire chapter from his notes.

One observant student once commented, "Well, if I have to go back and re-read my notes, then I'm reading the whole chapter twice." The answer is "Yes, but if you don't go back to internalize your notes, you'd be amazed how quickly you will forget them." Indeed, another curious characteristic about reading is how perishable the memory is. It's like a peeled banana; it starts turning brown within a few hours. If the student does re-read his notes, however, it may be the first time that student ever really read and understood a book—any book.

It is hard work to read a textbook chapter in this manner. The advantage is not only that a student now knows the facts that will be on the test, but that he has now mastered the method to read any narrative book or text he will need for the rest of his professional career. And it's not over. There's more. Now the student has to drill. Practice. Practice. Practice.

Practice

After reading and re-reading the entire chapter, a student may feel entitled to a break. He is. Indeed, after recalling all the important concepts effectively to prepare for the history test, a student probably is entitled to go out and engage in their favorite form of relaxation. Within a day or so, however, the serious student should come back to study the notes to more effectively imprint them in the brain. The final phase of internalizing the notes is simply to conduct exercises with them. This is simply re-writing them. For example, the student may choose to review the marginal notes in the chapter, and write them in outline form in a spiral notebook. Simply re-writing them will reinforce the mental impressions of the important concepts. He may even choose to list a few extra details for each concept. As stated above, many minor details can be recalled along with the important concept. After converting the marginal notes to an outline in the spiral notebook, the student may now wish to input the outline, line by line, into a laptop computer file. That not only deepens the mental impressions by writing again, but it now allows for digital massaging. In a computer, the student can now expand his keywords as whole sentences for all of the important concepts. He can now print out the expanded notes, and mark up the print-out with a pencil. After marking it up on paper, he can go back to the computer and input his penciled mark-up to edit his computer file. He can work and re-work his list of important concepts as much as he wants.

The obvious question is "How many times do you re-write your notes before the test?" The obvious answer is "As many times as it takes." It is demanding for a student to study this much and drill this much in a history textbook, but it is a simple process. It is hard work, but simple, like digging a ditch. Hard work, but so simple anybody can learn to do it. Thus, preparing for a history test is not so much a question of confusing facts. It's more a question of simple hard work. By the time a student has read and re-read a chapter and taken notes, he how has a vested interest in making all that work produce on the test. That justifies the practice, practice, practice. This completes the simple step-by-step method of reading to internalize the important concepts in a history textbook to identify the possible test questions. The only other step is using any resources or study guides available for the course. Study guides can be helpful, but they cannot substitute for the hard work described above. They should be used only after the step-by-step reading method, and only as an extra exercise after systematically internalizing the important concepts.

Study Guide

The study guide is just that, a guide to study. It is *not* a pre-test that assures you that if you can answer all the sample questions you will know the answers to a post-test. If you want the answers to the test, they are provided for you in the textbook, and only in the textbook. Your intensive work should not be focused on the study guide hoping to get clues. It should be focused on comprehensive reading in the textbook, identifying the important concept in each paragraph for the entire chapter. Spend your intensive work writing notes on those important concepts, and internalizing your notes. The only assurance you will get on a test is the assurance that you have made a list of all the important concepts in the chapter, and drilled yourself on them. The test is a test of those same important concepts you identi-fied in the textbook, and remember, you are smart enough to correctly identify 9 out of 10 of those concepts by using this method.

QUICK START: READING A TEXTBOOK

1. *Read* the chapter one paragraph at a time. Read a paragraph or subsection of the chapter. Stop. Don't read the next paragraph yet. Put the book down.

2. Stop to *synthesize* the content you just read in the paragraph or subsection. In other words, ask yourself, what did I just read? If you can't relate the main event or theme of the paragraph, go back and re-read it until you can discipline yourself to identify the main event or theme you just read.

3. As you synthesize the paragraph content, *identify* the important concept (the most important point). The paragraph may have many facts, but it will have only one important concept (main point). Identify it.

4. Write a *note* about the important concept in the margin of the book or in your notebook. The note should be only three words, no more. This is a note, not a sentence. You may want to underline (highlight) a name, a date, or a statistic in the paragraph as you read it, but do not underline more than a word. Don't underline a whole sentence or several sentences.

5. Now, move on to read the next paragraph or subsection of the chapter, and take a note for each paragraph.

6. After you have read and taken notes for each paragraph of subsection of the entire chapter, now go back and *re-read* the chapter a second time. This time, read only your notes in the margin. As you read a note, try to recall the details of the important concept. If you can't remember some detail, go ahead and re-read that part of the paragraph.

7. After you have read and *internalized* every note throughout the chapter, now go take a break. You deserve it after what should have been three to four hours of real college-level studying.

8. To study before the test, compare your important concepts to the items on the study guide for the chapter. Re-write your entire chapter notes in a notepad. And *drill* yourself, or get somebody else to drill you on your notes.

Notes

1. William E. Montgomery and Andrés Tijerina, *Building a Democrat Nation: A History of the United States to 1877,* Vol. 1, (Kendall/Hunt Publishing Company, 2010), p. 282.

CHAPTER II

Lecture Notes

    This chapter teaches you how to listen to a college lecture, take notes on it, and understand it well enough to pass a test on it. The chapter includes a one-page Quick Start: Lecture Notes attachment for those students who want to take notes on a lecture immediately. The Quick Start is a listening method that lets the student quickly identify the lecture facts that will be on a test. This is similar to the QUICK START on reading a textbook. It's for people who like to use a Quick Start when they open up the box of a brand-new computer and do not wish to wade through the thick Owner's Manual. Likewise, in a history lecture, a student can skip to the Quick Start first. But when they have more time to read a fuller explanation of how to really grasp the facts in a college lecture, students can read the full chapter.

INTRODUCTION TO LECTURE NOTES

    Lecture notes are the notes a student takes in class to remember the material in the professor's classroom lecture. Commonly, students write their notes by hand in a spiral notebook, but increasingly, students take their laptop computers to class to write their notes into a word processing file. It is necessary to take notes because the lecture covers such a great volume of facts, data, esoteric terms, or themes that a student could not practically expect to remember them all for a test. Also, the purpose of learning the lecture notes is primarily to prepare for the test. A test is based largely on the material covered in the lectures; therefore, it is to the student's advantage to remember, study, and be able to write the lecture material for the test. This chapter first identifies the important elements of a classroom lecture, and then it describes the basic steps to take notes in a way that will help the student to pass the test.

INTERPRETATION

The social sciences generally still use the lecture as the primary method of expository. The professor commonly uses a narrative or story line to describe events in history, to identify persons, or to describe historical trends. It may seem that these facts can be gained by simply reading a book, but a professor may provide intellectual stimulation, interactive discussions, and sometimes inspiration that cannot be gained by reading a book. One of the most important advantages of a lecture is the professor's own interpretation of the facts and events. An interpretation is like an opinion—a highly informed professional opinion. As an example, one professor may interpret that economic factors compelled the American colonists to defy British rule in 1776, although other scholars may disagree. They may believe instead that philosophical factors most strongly motivated the colonists.

The professor who interprets the economic reasons may be willing to accept that Americans felt insulted that they had to live under British rule, but that the insult was not enough to make them risk their lives. The professor's economic interpretation may be that paying taxes—even a few cents—every day for a pound of tea or sugar, did offend the American colonists to the point of rebellion. This interpretation argues that people will not necessarily rebel against theoretical principles, but they will fight to keep the little things in their daily life from changing. Is that true? Do you believe that people would actually rebel against the government over something as simple as the price of a gallon of unleaded fuel? A lecture can explain that the professor interprets those economic factors as being more important than ideas or theories. In the lecture, the professor can explain the particular interpretation and provide the reasons that make it more compelling than other interpretations. A student may not agree with the professor's interpretation, but sometimes students learn to be even more committed to their own opinion only after hearing the other side of the argument. Either way, the lecture helps the students to understand the professor's favorite interpretation. And there's no better way to get the professor's approval (goody points) than to quote the professor's favorite interpretation on a test or during a class discussion. It counts.

BIBLIOGRAPHY

Another advantage of the lecture format of teaching is that the student is introduced to a wide range of ideas and books about a topic. This is usually referred to as bibliography. Every course has a bibliography, just like a book has a list of books at the end. The bibliography identifies the books and sources that the author researched to write the book. Likewise, the professor's lecture mentions the books and sources that were researched to organize the lecture. The lecture allows the professor to present the list of books as evidence of the interpretation. For example, if a professor believes that American Indians were deceived by U.S. government agents, the lecture may mention Helen Hunt Jackson's *A Century of Dishonor*, on broken American treaties. The book is evidence to explain why the professor has this interpretation.

Students should write down the bibliography titles mentioned in a lecture for several reasons. Book titles may be on the test. A test question may ask "Which book most influenced the U.S. Congress to pass the Dawes Act to protect Indians from fraud?" Or the student may have to write an essay or research paper on the subject, and cite the book title as an example. Also, a student gains credibility by citing a book title to prove a point in a class discussion. Citing bibliography gives anybody credibility. Even in a Saturday night party crowd, people can quickly distinguish the windbag from the professional by the facts they state. One person spouts only biased opinion, and the other regularly cites evidence. A book title is the best evidence. It's bibliography. Bibliography is useful in the classroom lecture, on the test, and in life. Many professionals stock their office with their favorite books from college. It's not just their favorite college books; it's their credibility. In this way, the college history lecture offers a better list of books than any internet search.

SCHOLARLY CONCEPTS

The history lecture offers scholarly concepts that can be explained by the professor, using examples and discussion in the class. Scholarly concepts are ideas. They are complex ideas that are often so abstract and so theoretical that everyday conversation simply does not give a person time and freedom to discuss fully. The history lecture gives the student and the professor at least one hour of uninterrupted time in a quiet classroom to discuss all the parameters of a concept. The professor can define the topic, define its time period, indicate its geographic location on a classroom map, describe important persons, and explain several reasons for the actions that people took in the events. Most importantly, the history lecture provides an elaborate amount of evidence, documentation, and bibliography to explain the concept. All of the evidence and description are necessary because a scholarly concept is often abstract. It is not an event, but a theory about an event. An event, for example, may be the election of Andrew Jackson, but the concept may be that Jackson's presidency made the American people more democratic. The lecture provides example of the expansion of democracy, like the greater percentage of people voting, the proliferation of newspapers, and the growth of political parties. For the student in class, the scholarly concept is just another essay question on the test, but to the scholar, the concept may be an entire career of books and research. Jacksonian democracy, for example, is often taught as a 3-hour course in university upper-division courses. The lecture allows the college student to grasp a scholarly concept and see aspects of modern American politics that may never be perceived otherwise.

PHILOSOPHY IN THE LECTURE

The college lecture is the primary way for the student to learn the professor's philosophy. The professor is not actually there to explain the answers before the test, or simply to explain the subjects in the textbook. The professor gives lectures primarily to present the philosophy of the course. That is why the PhD history professor is not called a doctor of history but a doctor of philosophy. Students learn history from the textbook, but they learn philosophy in lecture. The textbook presents facts; the lecturer organizes those facts into a broad view of history. A textbook may explain, for example, that television is an electronic instrument which uses video images to convey a message. That is a fact. Marshall McLuhan may teach in a college lecture, however, that the American public is more impacted by the television imagery than by the message, itself. His philosophy may be that "the medium is the message." Such a philosophy would hold that Americans became a visually oriented nation as opposed to the old traditional hearing-oriented community. His philosophy is that Americans pay more attention to the image than to the person speaking. That philosophy may be the reason that John F. Kennedy defeated Richard Nixon after their televised debates in the 1960 presidential elections. Nixon tried to use words to convey his message, but he did not comprehend that by then, the American people were paying more attention to his drab TV image. By explaining his philosophy of television, Marshall McLuhan could convey this broader understanding in a lecture.

A course philosophy is one of the major advantages offered in a major university as compared to some smaller colleges, although students may not appreciate it. Students may complain that a major university history class is conducted primarily by a teaching assistant, rather than by the professor, who lectures only on a limited basis. Parents may complain that they prefer a "teaching college" that allows the teacher to focus on teaching the students. There are advantages to teaching, but the higher levels of college education may be achieved when a student comprehends an entirely new philosophy, and that is the goal of a college lecture. Students can read the facts in the textbook at home on their own, then go to the lecture to learn how those facts make up a philosophy. Multiple-choice questions on a test may ask for the textbook facts, but the broader exam questions usually ask a university student to articulate the broader philosophy. And that philosophy is presented in the professor's lecture.

TAKING LECTURE NOTES

Now that it has been established that the college lecture is a basic part of the history course, the student should take out a spiral notebook or a laptop computer, and start taking notes to learn the philosophy, the bibliography, the interpretation, and the many, many facts. The student has to follow important steps in taking notes because a 1-hour lecture has so many facts that the student cannot hope to remember them all unless they are written, studied, and organized into manageable cubbyholes or mental compartments. In taking notes, the student listens carefully to identify the key points, writes them down in an outline form, and organizes them for study before the test.

Step 1: Read the Textbook

The first step in taking good lecture notes is to read the textbook even before coming to class. As mentioned in Chapter 1, the textbook provides the basic facts for the course. But reading the textbook also stimulates the mind and serves as a prelude to the lecture. The advance reading plays an important role in making the mind receptive to learning the facts. This process takes advantage of a basic function of the mind's way of learning. The mind learns a fact better when it is already searching for that fact. It's as simple as opening the lid to a box before throwing something in. If you first ask someone a question, and they are already searching their mental database when you tell them the answer, they absorb it better. Their mind is receptive because you opened it with a stimulating inquiry. They get the fact, but it combines with the inquiry to make a relationship—a mental relationship. This makes a much deeper impression on the brain. It is important to deeply impress facts into the brain because when students get nervous during the test, they forget all but the deep impressions. This mental process is developed by first reading the facts in the textbook, and then hearing them in the lecture. Both senses—hearing and seeing—are critical in forming the mental relationship.

The classic quote of the ancient Chinese philosopher Confucius referred to this mental process over 2,000 years ago. Confucius said:

I hear and I forget. I see and I remember. I do and I understand.

He said he forgot things that he only heard, but he could remember things that he saw. That means a student who does not read the textbook first and comes to the lecture only hears it, and forgets it. Hearing dissipates quickly, like listening to a song on the radio. While listening to a singer reciting the lyrics, the listener enjoys the words, even mouths them along with the singer. But as soon as the song is over, the listener finds it is easy to "forget the lyrics." On the other hand, if the student hears something and then sees it in print, then it can be remembered. Did you ever hear somebody say they could spell a word better if they first wrote it down so they could see it? This may sound like empty theory, but the mind is visual in the learning process.

Consider the following scenario. A college student is invited to a party, and gets verbal instructions, "Go north on Lamar Street, turn left on 15th Street for two blocks, turn right, go one-half block to the alley, turn left, and it's the second garage apartment on the right, upstairs." Just about the time the partygoer hangs a right, the next turn may get confused with the alley turn. Compare this scenario with the same verbal instruction but now the student is handed a copy of a city map. The instructions are given verbally as a heavy red line is drawn on Lamar Street, a big "left" arrow at 15th Street, and a line all the way to the apartment, which is boxed with a large X. Would these instructions be easier to follow? Why? Because the mind now has a visual image to reinforce the verbal instructions. That is how the textbook can reinforce the verbal lecture in class. It provides not only the text, but the student's own study notes handwritten in the margins. The partygoer can now mouth the verbal instructions while looking at the map. That is how Confucius could remember also. He said, "I see and I remember."

Another everyday example of this mental process is experienced when somebody goes to see a movie that they've already seen once.

The second time they see the movie, they begin to notice things during the opening credits before the movie even starts. Not only do they notice the background details, but now they hear script lines that they missed the first time. They may even leave the movie afterward with a higher understanding of the theme of the movie or the hidden meanings in the movie title. So, when students go to the lecture, it should be like going to the movie for the second time. They should notice details in the lecture that they would not have heard if they had not first read the textbook. This way, they can read the textbook to prepare the mind for hearing the lecture. Sensory reinforcement is the simple but critical mental step. It is to the student's advantage to develop the study habit that facilitates the learning process by implementing these critical steps. First read, then hear the facts.

But Confucius actually went one step further. Confucius added, "I do and I understand." Confucius said he first forgets, then he remembers, and then he understands. How does Confucius understand? He understands by doing something. Doing what? He writes. The student writes. It's not enough to hear the lecture because you forget. You have to read the textbook to remember the facts. And finally, Confucius said that the mind has to do an activity—the student must write the lecture notes and do mental exercises with the notes. For example, you can drill, re-write the notes into a computer, or practice sample questions from the study guide. By doing study activities and exercises, you reach a higher level of mental cognition: understanding.

That's fine, but we still need to get our student home after the party. To use the third step by Confucius, consider the final scenario. Let the student actually drive. Put the student behind the wheel while being given verbal instructions and shown a city map of the route. As the student drives down the route, the verbal instructions are now being reinforced by visual images and the physical activity. Now, the student will learn the route so well that the map will not even be needed on the way home. That is the way you should prepare for a test. Read the textbook. Take lecture notes by hand, re-write them into a computer file, and do a practice exercise to drill on those notes. That's how to take lecture notes to pass history.

To review the study process, you read the book, listen to the lecture, and then you combine the textbook notes with the lecture notes and begins to see the broader issues in the history chapter. As your mind formulates the issues, the professor reinforces them with interpretations and books on the subject. And finally, you can begin to understand the higher concepts and the ultimate course objective, the philosophy.

This preparation may be a lot more complicated than the work that other students are doing. In fact, one of the most difficult challenges in reading a textbook is the peer pressure to avoid the textbook. A charismatic student in class may teasingly scoff at reading the textbook, or at even buying a textbook. Some may even boast about passing the course without reading the book at all. By comparison a conscientious student has to justify reading the textbook intensively, studying all night, and going to an early class to take notes. The reality is that some students might actually pass the course without studying this much—or they might not pass. They might skim by and pass the course with 1 point above passing minimum. Or they might miss one specific question that lowers their grade by 1 point below passing. They did not develop a comfortable margin of points above the minimum passing grade, and chance interfered. That is the problem with not studying. It leaves a 3-hour course grade to chance. The conscientious student is one who does not seek free time in college, but one who wants to know how to pass, with confidence. The reality is that both students are in the lecture for the same amount of class time, except that one student is absorbing about 4 times as much as the one who did not prepare for the lecture. It is not so much a matter of how much time as it is how well the time is used. The student conscientiously develops the study habits that facilitate the brain's learning process.

These are simple habits:

Read the textbook first.

Write specific notes.

Drill and internalize the notes.

Come to the lecture.

You will hear the same facts, but they'll make more sense now, especially when the professor narrates the historical events and weaves them into a scholarly interpretation.

Step 2: Listen for the Facts

The previous instruction has been to describe the general principles presented in the classroom lecture, that is, the philosophy, the interpretation, and so on. More specifically, the lecture provides information and key words that may point to or signal the important facts in the lecture. These signal terms may be on the test, or they may identify a fact that is on the test. The student should develop a keen listening skill to identify them in the lecture. One of the most obvious types of terms in a lecture is the glossary term. The glossary is the list of words, terms, proper nouns, and phrases provided as a study guide to help you learn these special terms. A glossary term is a word that may either be very unique or that may have a peculiar usage for the historical events in the textbook. For example, the word "packet" ordinarily refers to a bundle or package of goods, but in the history of early steamboats, it refers to the smaller steamboats that plied along the eastern seaboard of the United States in the 1830s. That term and its definition are peculiar to that chapter of American history. It would likely be listed in the glossary, and it would very likely be used in a multiple-choice test question. That is the reason that justifies listening for such terms and writing them down in the lecture notes. The glossary serves not only to signal the special terms of the textbook chapter, but also to provide the correct spelling. By studying the glossary terms, the student also has an opportunity to visually impress it in the brain for retrieval on the test.

One of the advantages of reading the textbook in advance and studying the glossary terms is not obvious. That is, simply that the student is already familiar with the words that the professor is using in the lecture. Knowing the glossary terms may not make the student stand out in class because the professor is simply using terms that the student read in the textbook, but that is the advantage. The student does not stand out. Some students stand out the wrong way. If a student has not read the textbook, and asks the professor to repeat a proper noun or a prominent name, like Aaron Burr, it may be rather obvious to the professor and the rest of the class that the student did not read the textbook. Likewise, if a student repeatedly asks the professor to spell a peculiar term, like "Blennerhassett," this may also reveal that this was the first time the student had encountered the term, which other students had already seen in the glossary. One of the most popular jokes among professors is the one about the student who wrote that "One of the causes of the Revolutionary War was the British put tacks in the tea." The student did not read the book. In the lecture, the student heard the word "tax," but thought the professor was saying "tacks." On the test, it became obvious that the student heard the lecture, but had not read the simple word "tax" in the book. This may not have actually happened in real life, but similar incidents are frequent in history class or test answers. They reveal that a student was using only the hearing senses to gain the facts, rather than visually studying the textbook as well. The student will probably not have points deducted for such a gaff, but he probably will not earn additional points on the test.

The glossary terms are the signals or the key words that point to the important facts in the lecture that will be on the test. Thus, by being familiar with these peculiar glossary terms, you can be more attuned to identifying the important facts. As an example, if you have already been introduced to the term "Blennerhassett" in the glossary, then you should more readily recognize it when you hear it in the lecture. And more importantly, you should also hear that Aaron Burr was involved in questionable activities on Blennerhassett Island. That fact is on the test. The process is that you first saw the key word or the glossary term in the textbook, and then identified it as a signal for the important fact in the lecture. Students often complain that they do not know what to listen for in the lecture. "What's important and what's not?" they ask. They ask because they did not read the textbook in advance. If you do read the textbook, then you can use the terms from the textbook to know "what's important." And just like the glossary terms, the notes that you wrote in the textbook can also signal important facts and important themes in the lecture. In the lecture, the professor often uses the same names, terms, and themes that you saw in the textbook.

By simply taking notes in the textbook first, you can have advance signals as a guide through the complex, intellectual lecture—and understand it. Most importantly, you can take notes on the facts that will be on the test.

Learn to identify the story that the professor is telling. In listening to the lecture, try to notice the order of the facts that the professor uses to construct a narrative or a story. The first part of a lecture is the historical context of the topic, that is, the setting. A professor starts a typical lecture by stating a topic or a theme just like a paragraph has a topic sentence. Later, the professor will lectures on that topic, providing all the facts, but first the professor typically describes the date, the geographic location, the major events, the important persons, and finally, the reason for the action. This is the who, what, when, where, and why. This basic information may be scattered throughout the one-hour lecture, but it may be in one leading sentence. For example, the professor may say, "The Erie Canal was established in 1825 by Governor Clinton to connect Lake Erie to the Hudson River." These are the basic facts of the topic, "The Erie Canal." Listen for them and write them down. They provide the historical context, or the setting for the topic. Next— listen for any detail, fact, name, or event on the topic of the Erie Canal. For example, how long it was, how much it cost, how the boats moved along the canal, and so on. These details are important because if they are not on a multiple-choice test question, then you should insert them as examples in an answer to a discussion question.

Facts are important in a history lecture. But students sometimes complain or ask "Will I have to know all the dates?" The answer is "Yes." They may seem like trivia, but dates are necessary to frame the chronological setting of an event. Just like your birthday. Did anybody ever ask your birthday? Of course. Almost every day. Dates fit the events together in a timeline. But dates do not tell the most important facts about a person. Your birthday does not say anything about your hard work in history class. It does not say anything about your ambitions, or your major course of study in college. Dates are like the other facts in a history lecture. They do not tell what is important about a subject, but they all combine to frame the historical setting of the subject, and that leads to the most important part of the lecture—the significance.

The significance is the lesson of the lecture. It is like "the moral of the story." It is the learning point that the professor wants the students to take away from the lecture. And it is the most likely point to be on the written mid-term exam or on the final exam. The significance is typically stated at the end of the lecture on a subject, and it tells why the subject is important in history. For example, at the end of the lecture on the Erie Canal, the professor might say, "The Erie Canal is significant because it was the model for other canals." It is like the "punch line" of the lecture, and it probably earns the most points on a test. You should listen for the significance of all major themes or subjects in the lecture.

To review then, in a lecture you should listen for the key words (glossary terms), important facts, dates, details, the major subject, the who, what, when, where, and why of each major subject, and finally the significance of each major subject. That's a lot to write, but it's a skill you need to develop.

Step 3: Write Complete and Accurate, Meticulously Detailed Notes

Listen for and write all the important facts in the lecture. A student must write all the important facts in a lecture while the professor is speaking. They may be written by hand in a spiral notebook, on loose leaf notebook paper, or in a laptop computer, but they must be recorded for later study. The notes must be complete, accurate, and meticulously detailed. So if the professor says that Europeans traded with the East for pepper, tea, cinnamon, and nutmeg, then you should write every one of those items in the notes. In order to do that, you must develop the ability to write all of those items while the professor continues to talk about another list of items. The first skill to develop then, is to be able to write complete, accurate, meticulously detailed notes while listening to the rest of the lecture. The worst part is that the lecture is fast and full of facts, names, dates, and statistics. How do you hear those other facts while still writing down "pepper, tea, cinnamon, and nutmeg"? Can it be done?

Yes. By first reading the textbook, writing those items in the textbook notes, and studying them the night before, so you are not overwhelmed to hear them in the lecture and are not wondering how to spell "cinnamon," because it was seen in the textbook. Can you learn to write copious notes while listening to the lecture? Yes. By diligently building the note-taking skills.

Before going any further, let's talk about building skills. This discussion and the time taken to build skills is a lot of extra work that other students don't have to do. Students who want average grades and easy courses do not have to do this extra work, and they never have to drill on special skills to read a textbook or to take lecture notes. That is true. But a student who is determined to pass a course does not leave anything to chance. Maybe you've already failed history twice, and now you need it to graduate. Maybe you need an A to keep a scholarship. Either way, you are like the doctor who wanted to become a brain surgeon specialist. He or she no longer uses a scalpel. Now he or she has to learn to use a microscopic surgical instrument. That is the process we all go through. You wanted to learn how to make an A in a college history course, so now you have to learn new skills and use new devices. So, you write faster, while you discipline yourself to listen to the professor at the same time. It's an advanced skill, and you can learn it. And just like riding a bike, you may stumble, but it gets easier as you progress. And once you develop the skill, you never forget it. Write down every detail, and write down the major significance of every subject in the lecture.

Now, another skill: Copy verbatim the keywords from the professor's blackboard notes. If the professor writes notes on the blackboard while lecturing, write those exact words into your lecture notes. Or, if the lecture includes a classroom projection screen, copy the exact words on the screen. Usually, these notes are bullet items in outline form. Use the exact terms in your notes. The reason to write these exact terms is that they are esoteric, that is, that they have a special meaning for this particular course. And they are succinct. They say a lot in one or two words. You could say them in your own words, or in a longer phrase, but it is to your advantage to use the professor's specific words. For example, if the professor says that Jacksonian democracy led to "democratization" of American politics, then write that exact word, "democratization." Also, use the professor's outline items in the same outline order as the professor's blackboard notes. One other reason to use the exact words is that most of those terms come from books written specifically about that lecture subject. A book on Jacksonian democracy, for example, may have been written by another scholar who is a national authority on the subject, and has a whole 30-page chapter defining the factors of "democratization" alone. Indeed, he may have coined the term in his award-winning book. It is only logical that a college student should learn from that scholar, and learn from the professor who is presenting that special word as part of the lecture. And, it will be on the test.

To review then—write the exact words, meticulously detailed, in the order and special wording as the lecture or the professor's black-board notes.

Step 4: Write Lecture Notes in an Outline

Lecture notes should be written as an annotated outline. They should be organized on the note page in sections. Each section of the outline should cover a major subject of the lecture. Within each section, the detailed facts of the subject should be written as subsections or indented lines under the main subject heading. Each line should be a phrase, not a full sentence, and not just a single word. Each indented line under each subject or section heading can be marked by a small symbol at the left margin. The symbol can be an asterisk, a dash, or a heavy bold dot called a "bullet." The bullet indicates that it is a single phrase. The outline, then, is a series of phrases or notes; thus, the term "annotated outline." It's an outline of notes. As the professor lectures on several subjects, you write another outline section for each subject. This organizes the entire one-hour verbose lecture into brief sections that can later be learned as separate parts. Each section has its related details. Organizing the lecture into sections helps to make the lecture content manageable. It reduces the content into short compartments of data that can be studied, memorized, drilled, and internalized.

Below is a sample of an annotated outline of a lecture on Jacksonian democracy:

Elections

- larger percent voted
- deeper population engagement with politics
- reflected rise in American spirits
- states used popular vote for presidential electors

Parties

- started using national party conventions
- established large party structures

Jackson's Victory

- by popular vote
- massive majority in South
- stood for removal of Indians from Gulf states

An annotated outline not only expedites note writing during the professor's lecture, but it also helps—to study it. You can learn each section as a unit, one at a time. The outline also helps you write the test answers. It helps you remember the multiple-choice answers, and it helps you organize a long written essay answer.

Step 5: Ask Questions

Learn to ask the professor questions during the lecture, if possible. Of course, asking questions may not be an option. Some professors do not provide students the opportunity to ask questions, or they may not encourage it. Some classroom configurations restrict a two-way interaction between the student and the lecturer. And many students are simply bashful or otherwise hesitant to display their confusion before a large class in a competitive environment. But—if there is an opportunity to ask questions during the lecture, it adds points to the test score. One clarification during the professor's lecture may well be the answer to a multiple-choice question on the test. This is your opportunity to ask the professor, "What is the significance of Jacksonian democracy?" Or in some cases, "Is this going to be on the test?" Students almost universally hesitate to stand up and ask a question before their peers, but professors almost universally appreciate a student asking a question on the higher understanding of the lesson. It demonstrates clearly that the student has complied with the professor's reading assignment, and it indicates that the student has studied beyond merely learning the facts. As mentioned in the previous discussion on Confucius, after drilling on the facts, you achieve a higher learning of the facts, and that is what professors appreciate being asked in class. "Did democratization in Jacksonian democracy spread democracy to all U.S. citizens, or just to the males?" There are different types of questions that you can ask in the lecture, but conscientious questions about the lecture is an inquiry that reinforces a correct fact. It is your right to inquire of a professor's lecture. And, finally, it is a skill that you need to develop to help you prepare for the test. Now, after all the questions and notes, you are left after a 1-hour lecture with too much writing to remember. How do you learn all those facts in several lectures for a test that will ask only a few questions?

Step 6: Study within 8 Hours

After taking pages of notes for the lecture, a student has to study those notes just as diligently as the textbook notes, and they have to be studied soon, because lecture notes can be forgotten just as quickly as Confucius said he forgot things he only heard. Likewise, the college student heard the history lecture. Now the brain will quickly forget what it heard. The lecture is the most perishable product in a history course. It's only verbal, unlike the textbook or the study guide. The textbook will last for 20 years. The lecture spiral notebook will fade after five years. But the lecture will dissipate from memory in less than eight hours. Just like the song on the radio—POOF—the eloquent words of a lecture spoil faster than a peeled banana. As soon as the professor dismisses lecture class, the words are gone. But it's worse than that. Even the student's written lecture notes will quickly be forgotten. That's right.

Within 8 hours after the lecture, your brain may find it difficult to remember the very facts that were written in the lecture notes. After a day or so, you may struggle to make sense of the phrases personally written by hand, especially if the lecture notes extended beyond one or two full pages. This problem is compounded if you allow several days or weeks to pass before re-visiting several pages of those extensive and detailed lecture notes. Earlier, it was stated that reading helps the brain rem-ember. This does not apply to writing. Lecture notes have to be studied within eight hours after the lecture, or they quickly dissipate. That means that after a full day of classes, the college student has to find a quiet study place, and read that day's lecture notes, line by line.

What??

As you read the first section of the professor's lecture, try to associate the detailed notes in the bulleted phrases within the section. Try to re-construct the major subject and its related facts. Write the significance of the subject along with the detailed facts. And finally, try to construct the whole subject into a manageable structure for mental storage. First, identify the topic sentence, then the who, what, where, when, and why, then the significance of the topic. Study each section of lecture notes in that three-part structure: the topic, the who, what, where, when, and why, and the significance.

TOPIC: The Erie Canal

DETAILS: Established in 1825 by Gov. Clinton to connect Lake Erie to the Hudson River.

SIGNIFICANCE: It was the model for other canals.

As you read and learn each section, try to remember the professor's discussion. You'll be amazed at how many details you can remember while you are looking at the day's lecture notes. Your brain will probably remember more than a computer hard disk. It won't recall as much data as a semi-conductor chip, but then a semi-conductor chip can't formulate the cognitive associations that your brain does instantly as it studies the day's lecture. As you formulate the several subjects of the lecture into your memory, you internalize the information for retrieval on the test two weeks from now. After re-constructing the entire lecture notes in your mind, then drill. Re-write them into a computer file. Do an exercise or have a roommate quiz you on your own lecture notes. This is the last step that Confucius said, in which doing helped him understand. As you do an exercise, you not only remember the notes, you begin to understand the lessons. You achieve a higher understand-ing of the lecture—the interpretation, the scholarly concepts, and the philosophy. Now, you're ready for the history test.

And now, go party. You deserve it. At the party, heaven help any-body who asks you what you've been studying because they're going to get an earful of Jacksonian democracy. For the next two years, you will know more about "democratization" than you want to remember. But it will be there, deeply impressed in your brain where you put it when you studied back in history class.

QUICK START: LECTURE NOTES

STEP 1: READ THE TEXTBOOK

Read and review your textbook notes the night before the lecture. You will hear the same facts, but they'll make more sense now, especially when the professor narrates the historical events and weaves them into a scholarly interpretation.

STEP 2: LISTEN FOR THE FACTS

Use the textbook glossary terms and your textbook notes as keywords to signals to the words and themes to listen for in the lecture.

STEP 3: WRITE COMPLETE AND ACCURATE, METICULOUSLY DETAILED NOTES

Write down every detail, and write down the major significance of every subject in the lecture. Copy verbatim the keywords from the professor's blackboard notes.

STEP 4: WRITE LECTURE NOTES IN AN OUTLINE

Write the lecture notes as an annotated outline. Write one section for each theme in the lecture. Under each section, write an indented line for each detailed fact marked by a small symbol like an asterisk, a dash, or a heavy bold dot called a "bullet." The bullet line should be a single phrase or note; thus, the term "annotated outline."

STEP 5: ASK QUESTIONS

Ask the professor to clarify anything that might be on the test, like "What is the significance of Jacksonian democracy?" Or ask specifically, "Is this going to be on the test?"

STEP 6: STUDY WITHIN EIGHT HOURS

As you read and learn each section, try to remember the professor's discussion. Internalize the information for retrieval on the test two weeks from now. After re-constructing the entire lecture notes in your mind, then drill. Re-write them into a computer file, or have a roommate quiz you.

CHAPTER III

Reading a History Book

This chapter teaches you how to read a history book and analyze it well enough to pass a test on it or write a book report on it. The chapter includes a one-page Quick Start: Reading a Monograph instruction for those students who want to start reading and taking notes on a history book. The Quick Start is a reading method that lets the student quickly organize the reading and take only pertinent notes. This is similar to the Quick Start on reading a textbook, except that the notes are on each book chapter instead of on each paragraph in the textbook.

INTRODUCTION TO READING A BOOK

A history book is called a monograph. It is a book that discusses only one major issue or event, thus, the prefix "mono" meaning one. It may be a book only on the Battle of Lexington. It may be only about Thomas Jefferson. The monograph represents extensive and detailed research and writing on one subject only. It is different from a textbook, which is comprised of hundreds of subjects and is taken from hundreds of monographs. Textbook notes have to be written paragraph by paragraph because each paragraph is about a different subject. Fortunately, notes for a monograph do not have to be written on each paragraph because the whole book is about only one subject. The monograph is read chapter by chapter, and brief notes are written only on each chapter. For this reason, each chapter monograph does have to be read and understood very well before reading succeeding chapters. And finally, the monograph has to be studied and understood because it may be part of a major exam, or because it has to be analyzed in a book report.

Scanning to Set a Learning Objective

Scanning a book is very popular with high school students because it is so simple and because it sounds like the teacher's permission to avoid the arduous task of reading. The procedures are simple: read the chapter titles, read the subsection titles, and look at the pictures. This simple description skips two important requirements. One is that you don't simply read the chapter titles and subsection titles. You have to mentally project their meaning and their relationship to each other. And second, you have to articulate the main subject or theme of the book. "Articulate" means put it into words, your own words, but think of the wording and putting your thoughts into words. That's different from simply looking at pictures. You should try to determine the lesson that the pictures were supposed to depict in the book. After reading the chapter titles and subtitles, for example, a student may think: "I think this book tells why Custer lost the battle because the title is *The Collapse of the Seventh Cavalry*, and the chapters describe how the officers misunderstood the general's orders to stay together." This is not simply conjecturing or guessing. It is projecting. It may not be accurate because the student has not really read the book yet. But it is an educated guess. And most important, it represents a hypothesis. It is a learning objective because, after you read it, you can go back to determine if your hypothesis was correct or not.

The purpose of a hypothesis is that it stimulates the reader's mind to searching for the true theme of the book. You set the hypothesis as a learning objective. In other words, you tell yourself, "I'm going to learn this about this book." You then read the book to determine if you were correct of not. If you were correct, and you projected the correct theme of the book, and you now can confirm it. If you projected wrongly, then you can now correct your hypothesis to read correctly. Either way, you confirm the correct theme of the book. The hypothesis helped you articulate the theme of the book, it helped keep you alert for the correct facts as you read the book, and it now reinforces in your mind, the meaning of the book.

I always remember my experience in seeing a movie entitled *Silence of the Lambs*[1]. I wanted to see the movie because I had worked on ranches in West Texas, and I expected to see lambs in the movie. I quickly learned that the movie had very little to do with fluffy little baby sheep. It was about a serial killer. The protagonist was an FBI detective named Clarice. As she pursues the killer, Clarice tells a story about her childhood when she visited a sheep ranch. She relates that she tried vainly to save the lambs from slaughter. This was the theme of the movie because she became obsessed with saving victims from criminals. As I heard her story in the movie, I realized that my hypothesis was wrong. But, I immediately identified the correct theme of the movie because I was actively searching for the theme. The value of a scanning a book and setting a hypothesis is not that you will necessarily set it correctly, but that you stimulate your mind to actively searching for it throughout the book. And when you see it, you will identify it correctly. That is why the object of scanning is setting a learning objective. It is your objective to not only scan the titles and chapters, but to give yourself a specific objective that you commit to learning in the book.

Another advantage to setting a learning objective is that it provides discipline and direction in a lengthy or even boring book. The analogy I use is like hunting a turkey a day before Thanksgiving. If you know you have to bag a turkey for the feast the next day, you don't waste time on a picnic in the woods. You quickly examine the terrain, and you go down the hills and into the valleys. You determine that a creek would attract prey, so you follow the creek downstream. You may see deer and rabbits along the way, but you don't waste time with them because nobody eats rabbit for Thanksgiving. When you see a turkey, you bag it and quickly exit the woods for home. You follow the creek back upstream, out of the valley, and up the hill to your vehicle. That's the way you have to enter a book. A book is like a forest, and you can get lost and go endlessly in circles unless you know what you are looking for. You can spend hours and hours reading the same paragraph over and over, and never get anything out of the book. You may say that the book was boring, but any book can be boring if you read in circles with no objective. With a specific learning objective, you go into the book, you identify the main theme, and you read the conclusion to get out of the book. Scan to set a learning objective. Set the learning objective, and start searching the book.

Read the Preface

The preface is like a short chapter where the author tells the purpose of the book. This is important because it tells you what the whole book is trying to prove. It is also important because it tells you what the book is not about. Either way, it helps to know the objective of the book. Sometimes the author says the purpose in clear, explicit terms like, "When I was a young girl, I noticed that books never told about women in the American Revolution. I wrote this book to demonstrate that women served not only to keep the family together, but they also served in the military campaigns." The author may even tell what the book is not about. For example, the author may add, "This book is not intended to glorify any particular woman or to determine the number of women who participated in the war." Or, in some cases, an author may use the preface to discuss major issues of the book, but never explicitly state the specific purpose. The readers are left with having to relate these issues to the rest of the book to try to make their own determination of the purpose of the book.

Write Notes on the Preface

After reading the preface, a student should write about four to five lines of notes on it. The notes may be in full sentences or in outline form with a major section on the preface and bullet lines under the section. As an example, the notes on the preface may be as follows:

PREFACE

Author says she grew up in New England and saw statues and read books about the American Revolutionary War

- never saw statues or read books about women in the war
- noticed the names of many women in the Massachusetts militia records, and wondered what role they played.

- Says she "wrote this book to demonstrate that women served not only to keep the family together, but they also served in the military campaigns." (p. xi)
- but "This book is not intended to glorify any particular woman or to determine the number of women who participated in the war."

Read Chapter by Chapter

Before reading a monograph, a serious student should establish a dedicated space and time for undisturbed reading. Just as previously discussed for reading a textbook, the college student should give serious attention to "the reading set up." Before reading a chapter, it should be scanned individually, noticing the chapter title, the chapter subsections, and the graphics. You should draw a hypothesis or a learning objective for the chapter based on the chapter title and the scanning, just as for the entire book. The learning objective should be an inquiry about the chapter title. For example, if the chapter title is "Dividing the Main Force: Major Reno's Attack," you may hypothesize that the chapter describes how the cavalry became divided before the battle. The subtitles and graphics such as sketches and maps in the chapter may reinforce or weaken the hypothesis. You should set a learning objective for the chapter, and read the chapter to prove the hypothesis. With such a conscientious objective, the reading of a chapter in a monograph is clearly not a pleasure exercise but a serious task to be accomplished with no wasted time.

Read Fast–Time Yourself

Time is a critical element in reading a history monograph. You should not only set a reading objective, but a timing objective as well. A major part of the reading set up is to use time efficiently. You may have a part-time job or a club meeting in the evening, and therefore must make the most of a two-hour period in the library. One way to do this is to set an objective to read a specified number of chapters in the two hours. First, read one chapter to determine your reading speed. For example, if you read 30 pages in one hour, then you know that your rate is two minutes per page, or one chapter each hour. Set your timing objective before reading the next chapter. Say, "It's now 7 PM. I'm going to finish Chapter 2 by 8 PM. Go." Start reading Chapter 2, and continually look at the clock to check yourself. If you are behind a page or two, then get back to speed.

Write Notes on Each Chapter

Read and write notes on all the chapters, including the epilogue, conclusion, and the bibliography. Reading all the chapters in a monograph may take one or two weeks if you have only 8 or 10 hours per week. But after all the chapters have been read, you should have notes for each chapter—about 5 to 10 lines per chapter. Chapter notes should include not only the main theme of the chapter, but any facts or quotes that may appear on a test or that may be needed to write a book report on the monograph. These include the following:

- An explanation of the meaning of the chapter title
- All important persons
- Notes on all major events, including the main dates for each
- The most important theme or lesson of the chapter

Study Your Chapter Notes

Within a day of finishing the book, go back and read the notes for each chapter until you internalize them. Remember to do some kind of exercise with your notes. For example, re-write them into a computer file or quiz yourself on the notes. Ask a friend or roommate to review your notes as you recite them aloud, chapter by chapter. This will help to impress the details and the major points into your brain. Treat each chapter like a major exam question that has a topic, details, and a major significant lesson, as if you had to be able to write them for an exam. After you have internalized or almost memorized the notes for each chapter, a brief mental review of your notes will allow you to draw certain conclusions about the monograph. For example, you may realize the author's purpose was fully accomplished in the book. You may begin to identify the author's major themes or arguments, and you may reach a conclusion about the importance of the book. You will most certainly have an opinion about the book and the author's writing style—thrilling, boring, technical, or readable. Write you own notes on your conclusions because you will use them all in the next phase of a college history course—the book report.

QUICK START: READING A MONOGRAPH

STEP 1: SCAN THE ENTIRE BOOK

Get a general idea of the major parts and subjects of the book by quickly looking at the book title, the table of contents, the chapter titles, the graphics, and the bibliography. Formulate a hypothesis of the book's major subject or point. For example, that the book is about how the United States made mistakes that lost the Vietnam War. The scan should take no more than 15 minutes.

STEP 2: READ THE INTRODUCTORY PAGES

Read the preface, the acknowledgements, the foreword, and the introduction to identify the author's specific purpose in writing this book.

STEP 3: WRITE NOTES ON THE INTRODUCTORY PAGES

Write about 4 lines of notes in your own words to describe the author's purpose if stated in the preface. Write notes on the main points from each of the other introductory elements.

STEP 4: SCAN THE FIRST CHAPTER

In 5 minutes, scan the first chapter to formulate an idea or a hypothesis of that chapter. Read the chapter title, read all of the subsections of the chapter, and look at the graphics. State or write in one sentence the major point that this chapter will make in the book. This is your learning objective for this chapter. After you read the chapter, you can decide how close you were to stating its main point correctly.

STEP 5: WRITE NOTES ON EACH CHAPTER

Write about 10 lines of notes on each chapter to tell in your own words what the chapter is about. Tell the major events, identify the major players, tell the time period, and especially explain the chapter title. Include prominent quotes. For quotes, write them verbatim, identify the person speaking, and include the page numbers of the quotes.

STEP 6: WRITE NOTES ON CONCLUDING SECTIONS

Write a few lines of notes on each of concluding sections like the conclusion, the epilogue, the endnotes, appendix, and the bibliography.

STEP 7: READ AND STUDY ALL CHAPTER NOTES

Within a day of finishing the book, read the notes for each chapter until you internalize them. Re-write them into a computer file or do an exercise to help impress the details and the major points into your brain. Treat each chapter like a major exam question that has a topic, details, and a major significant lesson, as if you had to be able to write them for an exam.

Notes

1. *The Silence of the Lambs*, prod. by Kenneth Utt and directed by Johathan Demme. Orion Pictures, 1991.

CHAPTER IV

Writing a Book Report

This chapter teaches you how to write a book report for a history class. The chapter includes a one-page Quick Start: Writing a Book Report attachment for those students who have already read a history monograph and want to start writing a report on it. The Quick Start is a series of steps or procedures for organizing the content and for editing and writing the finished product. Also included in this chapter are a generic outline and a project management calendar. The outline is to help organize the major elements of a book report and to initiate the revision process to the rough draft. The calendar is to plan the project procedures and to discipline the student to meet the deadline for submission. The purpose of this chapter is to propose a generic model of a book report which can be replicated for scholarly analysis of a history monograph by students in a lower-division undergraduate college history course. In addition to writing a quality product, the chapter also addresses project management, planning, and quality assurance as major elements of passing a history course.

BOOK REPORT SKILLS

The book report is a key product in a college lower-division history course. It is a critical exercise in the successful accomplishment and in the final grade of a history course. By utilizing writing skills, research, and analysis, the book report serves as an introduction to scholarship. Not only does it introduce the college student to research in online and hard-copy sources and journals, but it also provides for practice in formal writing. The book report allows you to practice literary analysis, identifying themes, formal grammar, writing style, and the maintenance of professional standards. Finally, the history book report introduces you to documentation standards such as footnotes and bibliography. You learn to rely on a professional reference book such as the Turabian *Manual for Writers* or the *Chicago Manual of Style*.

Step 1: Project Management

A book report is actually a project, similar to the kind of project managed by corporate or government professionals. Yes, a book report involves reading a book, but it also involves deadlines, planning and managing limited resources, and organization. You can take advantage of the opportunity to practice project management, and at the same time, organize a step-by-step list of procedures leading to a finished product in time to meet the deadline. The best part of project management is that it provides for built-in quality as it guides the student to meeting the deadline. In other words, it provides "quality assurance" of making an A by following the steps and doing them on time. The basis in project management is to design and write a calendar showing the date for each step of the book report project. The first step is to select and read the book as described in Chapter III Then, write a list of all the steps that include doing an outline, writing the first draft, revising, adding the footnotes and bibliography, and printing the final draft for submission on deadline.

After the list of steps or procedures is written in one column, then assign a date in a second column to the right of each step. Start entering the dates by assigning the due date to the last item. For example, you will write the due date next to the final step "Submit." In the example below, the due date is August 7. Now project backward to determine on which date a report due to be submitted on August 7 would be printed. It should be printed on August 6, so that's the date to enter next to "Print Final Draft." Proceed to assign a date to each of the other steps, working backward, putting a date beside each step, all the way to the first step of the project. Below is a sample calendar of a book report project.

PROJECT MANAGEMENT: BOOK REPORT

DATE	PROCEDURE
July 14	Obtain the book
July 24	Read the book (take notes)
	• Orient yourself to the book
	• Set a learning objective
	• Read chapter by chapter
	• Take notes on each chapter
	• Internalize your notes
July 26	Synthesize
July 29	Outline Lecture
July 30	Outline Exercise
July 31	Submit Outline
Aug. 1	Rough Draft
	• Print out
	• Review (mark up)
	• Revise on screen
Aug. 4	Write Subsequent Drafts
	• Repeat above steps
Aug. 5	Add title page, footnotes and bibliography
Aug. 6	Print Final Draft
Aug. 7	Formal Submit

A book report calendar is used to project the dates and the resources that will be used for a particular step in the project. For example, you will know to plan to use a computer printer on August 6, the day to print the final draft. You may be tempted to mentally plan these steps and not have to write the calendar. But it would be difficult to remember these details and doing them mentally would be leaving an important course grade to chance. By using the project calendar, you start training yourself in the procedures to be used later as a professional, one who cannot leave anything to chance.

Step 2: Outline

The most critical step in a book report is the outline. The outline organizes all the components and facts of a book report in the proper sequential order. It greatly facilitates the writing because it is easily converted from an outline of phrases into whole paragraphs of text for the report. Indeed, the outline solves one of the worst problems for many undergraduate students—procrastination. By making it so easy to write the rough draft, the outline lets you avoid the fear factor by telling you how to start the report. The outline dictates the first item to be written in the report; therefore, you don't have to ponder, "Where do I start?" You just write the first line of the outline, then the second line, and so on. The outline provides not only the order of the statements, but the structure of the entire report from beginning to end.

The outline structure is divided into 3 major sections: the introduction, the main body, and the conclusion. Each of these major sections has 3 components. That is a total of 9 components in the entire outline. Note that there is no other component to the outline and that the report does not include any other paragraphs or sections that are not included in this outline. Some other papers may require long, expressive essays about philosophy and lofty subjects like man's quest for world peace. But not this report. This is a basic report about one book and its author. For this outline, the student writes a brief note for each component and that completes the outline. There is nothing more.

Each component has a specific topic. Below is a generic outline with a topic for each component, followed by a paragraph to explain the component. Remember, the student writes just a brief note—not full sentences—with a few facts for each component.

SECTION 1: INTRODUCTION

Component 1: Purpose of Book Report

To analyze book (title), author, themes, and scholarship.

This is the report's opening sentence that states that the purpose of this report is to analyze the book and evaluate its scholarship. It names the title and the author, for example, "The purpose of this report is to analyze *The History of Florida* by George W. Smith, and to evaluate its scholarship."

Component 2: Author's Bio

Current position, expertise, bias, credentials, awards, other books.

This component describes the author's current title and position. It tells why the author is an expert in the subject, his highest college degree, and any book prizes he has won for this or other books.

Component 3: Author's Purpose

Stated in preface, implied, or unstated.

This is a note or a quote stating why the author wrote this book, for example, to show that women played a role in the American Revolution. It is best to use the author's own words in a direct quote if one was stated in the preface.

MAIN BODY

Author's distinguishing arguments; most important lesson.

The main body of the report lists the two or three main themes of the book. The themes are the main lessons that you learned by reading this book. You should cite one or two examples from the book for each theme. For example, if you learned that slaves were not bitterly angry, that is your major theme. You can cite examples of two slaves or events that made you realize that slaves were not angry.

continued

Component 4: Theme Statement #1

This component starts with a statement of the most important major fact you learned from this book. It should be worded as a statement, for example, "The main theme of this book is that African slaves were beaten frequently, but did not harbor deep feelings of hatred for their owners." Cite one or two examples that you read in the book. Give full descriptions and all the facts necessary to explain.

Cite two examples from the book.

Cite one or two examples of this theme that you read in the book. Give full descriptions and all the facts to explain how they illustrate your theme. For example, tell how one particular slave continued to love his master even after emancipation. Give the names, dates, and details that show your point. Then cite another example to further support your theme.

Component 5: Theme Statement #2

This component is a statement of the second most important theme. Cite one or two examples that you read in the book, and give full descriptions and all the facts to explain

Cite two examples from the book.

Cite one or two examples of the second major theme that you read in the book. Give full descriptions and all the facts to support your theme.

Component 6: Theme Statement #3

This component is a statement of the third most important theme. Cite one or two examples that you read in the book, and give full descriptions and all the facts to explain

Cite two examples from the book.

Cite one or two examples of the third major theme that you read in the book. Give full descriptions and all the facts to support your theme.

continued

CONCLUSION

Component 7: Analysis

This component is simply a list of descriptive sentences about the book.

Genre, style, method, sources, author's success proving argument

This component is simply a list of descriptive sentences about the book. First identify the genre or type of book you read. For example, state if it is a biography, a narrative history, a legal analysis, a compilation of interviews, or a series of printed interviews. Next, describe the method used by the author, for example, a legal analysis, a sociological survey, or a descriptive story. Describe the type of books or sources the author researched in writing this book, for example, old newspapers, live interviews, archival documents, or secondary sources and published books. Finally, state whether or not the author succeeded in accomplishing the purpose stated in Component 3 above "Author's Purpose." State that the author did or did not succeed in proving that point, and tell why you think he succeeded.

Component 8: Book Review

A single phrase, 2 to 3 sentences encapsulating reviewer's opinion.

Read a book review written by a professional historian or reviewer, and use one brief phrase from that review, "The best book on the subject." Try to cite the reviewer's name, title, and the publication if possible in your statement, for example, "John Smith, distinguished historian of Yale University, stated in the *American Historical Review* that the is 'the best book on the subject.'"

Component 9: Your Opinion

Recommendation, what you like/dislike; how it impacts the reader.

The educated opinion has 3 parts. You should make a simple statement that you like the book or that you did not like it. You should state the reason that you liked it or not. And finally, you should state how it impacted you. For example, you can say, "The book makes a believer that slavery was an evil institution."

Step 3: The Annotated Outline

Below is a sample of an outline that has been annotated with a student's own wording of notes for each of the 9 components:

ANNOTATED OUTLINE

I. INTRODUCTION

1. **Purpose:** To analyze and identify the major themes of Gary Anderson, *Conquest of Texas: Ethnic Cleansing in the Promised Land*; to contrast themes w/textbook and other authors.

2. **Author's Bio:** PhD University of Toledo, 1978; Professor at Univ. of Oklahoma; other books on Indians include *Sitting Bull*, *The Indian Southwest,* and *Little Crow.*

3. **Author's purpose:** To present a "new paradigm for understanding the violence" as ethnic cleansing.

MAIN THEMES

4. **Main Theme #1:** "rather than a fight for liberty, the 1835 Anglo-led revolution was a poorly conceived southern land grab" and was used to expand slavery (p. 5)

   • Edw. Burleson destroyed Kichai Caddo villages on Trinity (1835).

   • Houston's treaty with Cherokees collapsed.

5. **Main Theme #2:** Land speculators spread massacre rumors to draw U.S. into war with Mexico.

   • Gen. TJ Green's rumors Mexico incited Indians attacks (p. 22).

   • Gen. Gaines asked for funds and twice brought U.S. troops.

6. **Main Theme #3:** Comanches retaliated during the Revolution with numerous bold attacks.

   • Comanche land claims were ludicrous to the Anglo-Texans.

   • Captive narratives led to Anglo reprisals.

CONCLUSION

7. **Analysis:** Narrative history of Indians by authority; succeeded in purpose; used archives of Mexico, U.S., and Texas.

8. **Book Review** by Andrés Tijerina in *A.H.R.* (Dec. 2006, p. 1512) says "successfully argues ethnic cleansing."

9. **Opinion:** Necessary read, other side of Texas Indian wars, sympathy.

Step 4: Rough Draft

The rough draft is the student's first attempt to write the report. It is called a "rough" or exploratory draft because it has not been refined or corrected. Other versions of the report will be revised to correct any misspelled words or poor grammar. It is important that those later versions be correct. However, it is just as important that this rough draft be "rough." As the student starts to write the rough draft, it is important to avoid the temptation to correct the spelling and grammar. The most important objective in writing the rough draft is to write it quickly and complete it in only a few pages. The reason for the quick draft is that it allows the student to continue immediately to the next step. This is critical. Otherwise, the average beginning writer quickly bogs down into a quandary of minute details that stop all progress. The writer is tempted quickly to ponder, "Should I say it this way, or should I use another word?" This pondering and hesitation leads to doubts and fear of writing the "wrong" word. That is the birth of procrastination and "fear of writing." It chokes the best writers.

This is the reason that the outline and the rough draft are so important. They allow the student to be sketchy and brief in the notes for the outline—no deep thoughts or special words. The rough draft also allows the student to be imprecise, even sloppy, with no penalty or fear of criticism. This freedom to write is the key to writing a report and passing a history course. It is just as important to professional writers. All of us have fear of writing. It is natural to procrastinate. One of the best signs of people who have a deadline to meet is that they spend an hour cleaning up every pen and pencil on their desk. It is their way of avoiding the frightening decisions of "Where do I start?" It is important for a student to learn skills to avoid the pitfalls that plague all writers.

A famous writer, Barbara Tuchman, explained in the preface to her Pulitzer Prize–winning classic book that even she also has to discipline herself to finish each step of the writing process. The research, the writing, the wordings—all must be finished quickly, she advises. Indeed, Tuchman admits that she intentionally does not finish any of them. She works on them for a sufficient time, and quits before she finishes a step. She actually moves on without finishing a step. The reason is not that the step is not complete. It is complete enough to win her a Pulitzer Prize. The reason is that if she waits until she is comfortable, she will never quit because a writer is never comfortable. In her preface, Tuchman said, "One must stop before one has finished... otherwise, one will never stop and never finish." She adds, "writing is hard work."[1]

For the undergraduate college student writing a book report, this means that the outline must be quickly written with brief notes, and the rough draft must be just as quickly done with quick, sloppy mistakes—but done. Finished. And, after the rough draft is finished, then, the serious decisions can be made about selecting just the right word, spelling correctly, and using perfect grammar. The best part of all this is that the rough draft is one of the easiest steps of the book report, and the most gratifying. How can writing a three-page draft be gratifying?

The reason a rough draft is so critical and so easy is that it is nothing more than the same annotated outline that the student just finished, only it is re-written in full sentences. In other words, where the outline says the author's biography is

Author's Bio: Ph.D. University of Toledo, 1978; Professor at Univ. of Oklahoma; other books on Indians include *Sitting Bull*, *The Indian Southwest*, and *Little Crow.*

the student simply writes that note as fully articulated sentences with all the *and*'s, *but*'s, and *the*'s. For example, the above note would be written

> The author received his PhD from the University of Toledo in 1978 and is now a professor of history at the University of Oklahoma. His other books on the subject of American Indians include his book *Sitting Bull*, his book *The Indian Southwest*, and his other book *Little Crow*.

A simple way to do this on a computer word processing program is to place the cursor in front of a line of the outline and re-write that line as a full sentence. Then re-write all the other lines of the outline as full sentences. During this process, the student writes quickly, with stopping to get it perfect, remembering Barbara Tuchman's advice, "Stop correcting it, or you'll never finish." One exception to this advice is that the student should write full explanations of the notes. This means to write not only fully articulated sentences, but many sentences for all the brief notes in the outline. For example, where the outline says

> **7. Analysis:** Narrative history of Indians by authority; succeeded in purpose; used archives of Mexico, U.S., and Texas.

the student writes several full sentences to fully explain all of the details. Notice below that although the sentences may have a misspelled word or awkward wording, they fully expand the brief notes into a full paragraph:

> *Conquest of Texas: Ethnic Cleansing in the Promised Land* represents a narrative history of the American Indians written by a distinguished historian, anthrapologist, [sic] and writer. Gary Anderson, a professor at the University of Oklahoma, clearly succeeded in his purpose in this scholarly work. He established a new paradigm for understanding the violence experienced by the American Indians as ethnic cleansing. [sic] The book's bibliography clearly shows makes it clear [sic] that Anderson made extensive use of the archives in Mexico, the United States Library of Congress, and the archives of Texas at the State Archives in Austin and at the University of Texas at Austin.

By re-writing each note into a full sentence, the student quickly converts the outline into a three-page draft. It may have misspelled words and other minor errors, but it is finished, and it can now be refined and revise to produce a cleaner draft. This is the revising process.

Step 5: The Revisions

The revision process is a series of steps to re-write the draft several times, each time making minor corrections until the final draft is complete, well worded, and free of errors. Save a file of each new draft in the computer with the latest corrections or revisions. To begin the process of revision, first print out the "rough draft" on hard-copy paper. Read through it. As you review it, mark up every error or misspelled word in the rough draft hard copy. Use preferably red ink to correct or mark up every misspelled word, grammar mistake, or other poor sentences. Put that marked up hard copy in front of your computer, and re-type every red mark correction into the rough draft on the computer screen. After entering all the corrections, this converts the rough draft into a corrected draft. Now you can save this corrected or revised draft as "second draft." In other words, use the save as feature to create a new version of the draft labeled as "second draft" in the computer. Now that you have the second draft saved, take a break. After the break, come back and repeat the steps above to print out the second draft and save the corrected version as "third draft." Repeat these steps for the "fourth draft" and as many drafts as necessary until you can find no more misspelled words, grammar corrections, or errors.

It is helpful to enlist the help of your peers in the revision process by asking them to review and mark up one of these versions. Other people can sometimes see mistakes that we cannot see in our own paper. A roommate, an English professor, or a parent can sometimes be enlisted as a reviewer. Remember to give them ample notice and time to do the revisions because they may not have time to do it immediately. Take their mark ups and comments amiably, even though some people may be a bit harsh in their remarks about your literary work. After satisfying yourself that you have refined your report to the standards necessary to receive an A on the assignment, then save as "final draft." At this point the footnotes, bibliography, and title page can be added to complete the report.

QUICK START: WRITING A BOOK REPORT

STEP 1: PROJECT MANAGEMENT

Design and write a calendar showing the date for each step in organizing and writing the book report from the first day the book is read until the last day that the report is submitted. First, list all the steps, and then put a date in front of each step. Start by putting the due date on the last item, and work backward, putting a date beside each step, all the way to the first step of the project.

STEP 2: STUDY MONOGRAPH NOTES

After reading the monograph and writing notes for it, study intensively all of the notes for each chapter of the monograph until you internalize them. Learn the notes for each chapter as if you had to be able to write them for an exam.

STEP 3: WRITE EACH STEP OF THE OUTLINE

Write in your own words, notes to yourself on each of the nine elements of the outline. The outline should be no longer than one page long, but as detailed as possible. It should include any direct quotes, special details or names, and page numbers to indicate where footnotes will later be inserted. Notes should be detailed enough that anybody could construct a full sentence from the note, without having even read the book.

STEP 4: THE ROUGH DRAFT

Put the computer cursor at the front of the first line of notes in the outline, and re-write that note as a full sentence with all articles, conjunctions, appositives, and punctuation. In other words, convert each note into at least one complete sentence, if not two or three sentences, fully articulated. Write in a footnote superscript numeral everywhere a footnote will be inserted. After converting the entire outline to full sentences, the outline should now be a fully written rough draft. Now save as "First Draft."

STEP 5: REVISE

Print out the first draft in hard copy. Mark up the first draft hard copy, using red ink to mark every misspelled word, grammar correction, or error. Put that marked up hard copy in front of your computer, and enter every red mark correction into the first draft on the computer screen. This should convert the first draft into a corrected draft. Now save as "Second Draft."

STEP 6: REPEAT REVISIONS

Repeat Step 5 for succeeding drafts. Print out the second draft. Mark it up in red ink, enter the corrections on the computer screen. Save as "third draft." Repeat these steps for "fourth draft" and as many drafts as necessary until you can find no more misspelled words, grammar corrections, or errors. Save as "final draft."

STEP 7: ADD ENDNOTES, BIBLIOGRAPHY, AND TITLE PAGE

Write the endnotes and bibliography pages, and add them to the back of the final draft. Attach the title page to the front of the final draft.

STEP 8: SUBMIT

Print out and bind the report a day before it is due, and set it aside. On the due date, submit the report.

Notes

1.   Barbara W. Tuchman, *The Guns of August* (New York: Ballantine Books, 1962), p. xi.

CHAPTER V

Research

RESEARCH FOR A TERM PAPER

This chapter teaches you how to conduct the research for a report or term paper in a college history course. It reviews the basic rules typically followed when writing a research paper, and includes a few procedures to do the actual research. A research paper is a formal report that a professor assigns each student to do during the semester for a major percentage of the course grade. The professor usually assigns or approves the subject for the research paper, but sometimes you can request a subject that provides background for your major field of study. In selecting your subject, it is important to review the availability of books, documents, and other sources of information on the subject in your college library or other local libraries. The student is expected to conduct independent research, and to write a report including footnotes and a bibliography.

A typical college report is approximately 1,800 to 2,000 words long, which is about 8 to 10 double-spaced printed pages, including the footnotes and bibliography. For this reason, you should be able to compile several pages of notes from the internet and from books and other hard-copy documents. Make an effort to use hard-copy books as much as online sources for research on your paper. It is easy to use the internet, but the information online is often generic and superficial. A college-level history project like this is intended to introduce you to special viewpoints or insight on an issue. A book may be harder to find in a library, but it will take you into corridors of thought you would never have pursued otherwise. Use your college course experience expand your horizons.

SOURCES: PRIMARY AND SECONDARY

One of the typical requirements in a term paper is the use of primary sources and secondary sources. A primary source is a document that was written by someone who lived at the time or took part in the event described in history. A primary source may be a letter, a diary, a newspaper, a daily log, or a government document that was written or published at the time in history that they were writing about. The Declaration of Independence, for example, is a primary document, but so is Thomas Paine's *Common Sense* because both were written at the time of the American Revolution. These may be found in library archives, and they may be rare. However, many primary sources have been reprinted or published in modern books, which are much more readily available. A published diary, for example, is a primary document because it was originally written at an early historical period, even if it were published only recently. The same is true of a recent reprint of Paine's *Common Sense*. It is still a primary source even if the reprint is new. Many original documents are now available on the internet, and may be used to meet the primary-source requirement of a term paper. For example, the Library of Congress has hundreds of recorded interviews of Americans in the 1930s, which are excellent primary sources.

Secondary sources are books and articles written at a later time, usually by historians or editors who did not necessarily live at the time of the event in history. For example, a history of the American Revolution written and published in 1995 is a secondary source because the author wrote it long after the event. The book and be a modern author's interpretation and analysis of the event, but it was not written in 1776.

The advantage of a primary source is that the writer may have actually witnessed the historical event, and had first-hand knowledge of the event. Being a witness to an event gives a person credibility in writing about it. It makes their account more believable than a person writing about it 100 years later. Also, a primary source may be more factual. A police log or a cargo register may list only names of individuals or a number of boxes with simple descriptions. But the register may have recorded the date and location, and a register is usually signed to certify the truth and accuracy. These features give strong evidence of the truth of the document, and make your term paper much stronger than secondary sources or mere opinion. It is usually best to include a few primary sources along with the secondary sources and books for your term paper.

Now, you may ask "How do I know which books and documents to research?" The first step in searching sources is to start with a common, readily available book by a reputable author on your subject. Read it. Then, make a list of book titles from the sources listed in the footnotes and bibliography of that book. This is called an extended bibliographic search.

EXTENDED BIBLIOGRAPHIC SEARCH

The easiest way to identify the books and sources to search for your term paper is to use the sources already used by an expert historian in your subject. For example, if you are doing a research paper on the Battle of Gettysburg, find a popular book on the Civil War, and identify the sources used in that book for the pages describing the Battle of Gettysburg. The best method is to find the footnotes in the pages describing the battle. Those footnotes provide the exact titles and locations of the books and other sources, including page numbers. Also, the bibliography or list of sources at the end of that book may also identify the specific book titles and sources that the author used in writing on the Battle of Gettysburg. By looking through the footnotes and bibliography of a popular book, a student can quickly compile a list of titles and sources on a specific subject. Your list should include the author's name, the title, publisher, date of publication, and page numbers. For primary sources and documents, the list should include not only the title of the document, but also the library where it is held. A copy of a court document, for example, may be listed as filed in the university archives. If you use a source that is available online on the internet, the document title and URL code should be listed with the title.

The list that you compile from the footnotes and bibliography of one book can then be augmented with titles from other books. You can find a another book on the subject, for example, a second popular book on the Civil War, and search that second book for the footnotes on the Battle of Gettysburg. Compile the book titles and sources in that book to add to the list from the first book. By going to other books, you "extend" your bibliographic search—your search for books. After compiling a few titles from two or three popular books on the Civil War, you develop a growing list of titles and sources on the Battle of Gettysburg. Now you can extend your search one further level up.

To extend a bibliographic search further, you can now go to the library to look into the books that you found listed in the first book's bibliography. Open one of those books, look in that book's bibliography, and find additional titles on the Battle of Gettysburg. Each book should add a few new book titles. This is the simplest method to find and compile your list of books and to extend the list of sources for your research paper. Also, just as you can find popular books on the Civil War to scour for your bibliography list, you can find articles on the Battle of Gettysburg published in scholarly journals or magazines like the *American Historical Review* or *American Heritage* magazine. The major scholarly journals have been published for over 100 years, and may have hundreds of articles on a subject like the Civil War. Scholarly journals and magazines are found in college libraries along with the books. To find a subject in a journal, you search the index of that journal for your subject, "Battle of Gettysburg." The index identifies the year, the volume number, and the page of the journal for your article on the Battle of Gettysburg. A 30-page article in the scholarly journal often has as many book titles and primary sources on your subject as a major book because the entire article may be related to that one subject.

After compiling and obtaining your list of books and sources from the extended bibliographic search, read through them to extract any relevant and important facts for your research paper. By citing an extensive list of sources—primary and secondary—a college student demonstrates a broad search and an extensive survey of research on the subject. In other words, it shows you "did your homework" before writing the report. After compiling a list of book titles and primary sources, you must narrow the list down to the books and sources that are actually available to you. You probably cannot go, for example, to the Library of Congress in Washington, D.C. to read a primary document, but you might be able to find another one from your list at the local college library archives. Make a list of those that are available to you, and begin a systematic search through those books and sources—one at a time—to extract the information on your subject. As you peruse these books, take accurate notes. You will need accurate research notes to write your research paper.

RESEARCH NOTES

As you read through several books and primary source documents on your subject, you compile such a massive amount of data that you must organize it into manageable records. These are your research notes. You will need two types of research notes: bibliography notes and content notes. A bibliography note is simply a note on the title of a book you used in your research. You should write the author's full name, the title and subtitle, the publisher, city, and date of publication for each book or article. Primary sources use a little different format, but they should also be recorded in your bibliography notes. A formal bibliography will probably be required for the term paper, and it typically requires the full title and publication information on each book and source you used. The preferred form for the bibliography in a history report is found in Kate Turabian's *A Manual for Writers of Term Papers, Theses, and Dissertations*, located in most libraries.

The content notes are any facts or quotes that you copy from the books that you use in your term paper. A content note is usually a paragraph or two in your own words to record a fact. If you use a quote from a book, be sure to write it verbatim—word for word—because you will need to put it in quotation marks in your report, and you must also attach a footnote with the exact page number where you found that quote. As you compile your research notes, they may become bulky and disorganized. It is necessary to use a system for organizing your research notes. This may be either hard copy or electronic.

If you choose to write your research notes by hand on paper, it is best to use a 3 × 5 inch index card for each note. Separate the bibliography cards from the content cards and then separate the content cards by topic. If you choose to use a computer to record your research notes electronically, this can be done on a page of text in a word processing file, in a spreadsheet file, or as separate records in a data base. All notes should include complete citation data.

Sample of index content card:

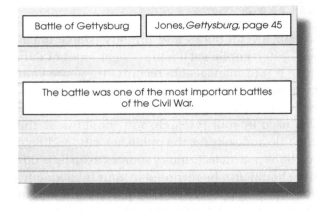

Battle of Gettysburg   Jones, *Gettysburg*, page 45

The battle was one of the most important battles of the Civil War.

CHAPTER VI

Online History Course

This chapter is for students who take one of the growing number of college courses conducted primarily by computer on the internet, the online history course. An online history course is a standard college history course, usually a lower-division undergraduate course on American history or a common survey course for transfer to a major university. The course is often taken by the student at home on the computer, independently and with little or no personal meeting with the professor. This chapter reviews some of the common activities that students are required to do, along with suggestions for successful accomplishment.

On online history course is usually a self-paced version of the standard American history survey course. It typically requires the same amount of work with the same quality standards and grading as a standard college classroom course. It requires independent work by the student. It is often self-paced; that is, the student reads the course syllabus on the course web page, follows the instructions, reads the textbook according to the scheduled assignments, and takes the tests online or at a proctored testing center. This necessarily requires unlimited access to a computer and the internet, and a very mature college student.

ONLINE CONTACT

One of the first requirements in taking an online course is for the students to communicate with the professor electronically, either through the course web page or through e-mail. When communicating course information with the professor, students must consistently identify themselves to the professor on every contact. In an e-mail message, for example, you should always write your name, course, and section number in every message. The e-mail subject line should quickly identify your required procedure. For example, your e-mail return address should clearly include your full name as listed on the official college admissions enrollment roster. Your first line in the message should state your course and section number like "History 1302, Sec. #25841," and your subject line should state your purpose, such as "Reporting Test #2 complete."

Failure to cite your name and course information may mean your message is deleted as junk mail. Students are responsible for effective communication with the professor in an online course, and usually will not receive credit for a message that does not clearly identify them by name. If a student's e-mail message is lost, misdirected, or deleted, the professor is not required to allow that student to take a test over. The student should ask for some indication either by reply e-mail message or on the electronic course web page that the professor received a required contact or report; otherwise, the professor's e-mail reply may be the student's only confirmation that the message was received on time as required. If the student submits a report through an e-mail attachment, and never receives a reply, the professor has no way of knowing that the student actually submitted it. In such a controversy, the student may not be allowed to submit another copy, especially if a deadline has passed.

Reading and following the procedures on a course syllabus are critical in an online course. The syllabus provides specific instructions for the grading method and requirements, the posting of the grades, and the calculations for each letter grade. The syllabus usually specifies the title of the textbook and the edition, which are critical for studying and testing purposes. If the student buys the wrong edition of the textbook, the study guide and the tests may not be numbered the same as the required textbook edition. The chapters in the 8th edition of the textbook, for example, may be different from the chapter numbers in the 9th edition of the same textbook. The student should read the syllabus meticulously, underlining or highlighting important dates and details.

An online course involves an inherent security risk because of computer hacking and because of the anonymity of the user. For example, the professor has no way of knowing the identify of a person sending an e-mail or submitting a report. Federal laws guard the confidentiality of student records. They prohibit a professor from releasing a student's grades or course progress online, except through password-encrypted web pages. A student should not expect to receive grades by e-mail, or to have a friend or parent obtain a course grade from the professor by e-mail. Students should make the e-mail contact personally, and use the course encrypted web pages for all online course contacts.

STUDY GUIDES

Many online courses include a study guide to provide a review of textbook content before the test. The study guide is usually a chapter-by-chapter list of questions or learning objectives for the entire textbook. The questions typically identify the facts that the student should have learned in reading the textbook. These are called learning objectives. They are often written as questions to query the student for specific facts. For example, a learning objective may ask the student to identify three products listed as "enumerated goods" in the English colonies. The student should be able to answer this question based on an effective reading of the textbook, and also to determine if the student is prepared to take a test on the material. You should not attempt to use the study guide as a pre-test, and don't assume that it guarantee knowing the answers for the test. The answers are in the textbook, not in the study guide. You should read the textbook first, take notes, study your textbook notes, and then review the study guide.

The study guide is just that, a guide to study. It is *not* a pre-test that assures you that if you can answer all the sample questions you will know the answers to a post-test. If you want the answers to the test, they are provided for you in the textbook, and only in the textbook. Your intensive work should not be focused on the study guide hoping to get clues. It should be focused on comprehensive reading in the textbook and identifying the facts in the textbook. Spend your intensive work writing notes on those important concepts and internalizing your notes. The only assurance you will get on a test is the assurance that you have made a list of all the important concepts in the chapter, and drilled yourself on them. The test is a test of those same important concepts you identified in the textbook.

DEADLINES

Students are responsible to meet deadlines for reading assignments, book reports, and tests in an online course. You should familiarize yourself not only with the dates, but with the requirements for each deadline. For example, an online course may require that a test be taken before a date or on a specific date. It may require that t a report be submitted on a specific date, or that the professor's reply for a report be received by that date. Tests also have to be taken by specific deadlines. The penalty for missing a deadline is usually failure for the requirement. You should plan a course schedule in advance to avoid conflicts that may interfere with taking a test on the deadline.

CHAPTER VII

Testing

This chapter reviews basic skills for taking and passing a history test. A history test, like a history textbook, is different from a test in other disciplines in that it usually requires the student to correctly identify facts. Even a discussion question on a history test requires the student to know facts and be able to analyze or interpret them. The student should study and internalize the important facts in the lecture and the textbook in order to be ready to use those facts to answer the questions and pass the test. This requires that students take their textbook notes and lecture notes in a form that prepares them for the test. It requires that students organize their notes, prioritize the facts, and study regularly during the week, long before the test.

ORGANIZING BEFORE THE TEST

Successful testing begins weeks before the test. It begins while the student is reading the textbook assignment, and while the student is taking lecture notes in class. While the student is reading the textbook, the student should be identifying the important concepts that may be on the test. By comparing the important concepts in the textbook to those important concepts noted in the class lecture with the learning objectives on the study guide, the student can compile a list of prospective test questions. For example, if the "enumerated goods" are noted in the textbook reading, and they are mentioned by the professor in the lecture, and they surface again as a learning objective in the study guide, then that repetition indicates that they will be a question on the test. The "enumerated goods" should be placed on a list of prospective test questions. Students are not commonly provided with a list of the questions before a test, but they are given many clues and indications if they are alert during the lecture and textbook reading. Compiling a list of prospective questions is one skill that a college student can develop. Studying that list is another skill. Discussing that list with the teaching assistant or the professor in advance is another skill that may be available to assertive students. The most important skill is regularly studying the learning objectives and facts during the weeks before the test instead of waiting until the night before the test to cram in the late night hours.

Another important part of testing is the essay question. This is actually not an essay because it does not involve the student's opinion. It is actually a discussion question because the student is asked to discuss a major issue in history. As mentioned in a Chapter II, the lecture provides an excellent format for the professor's narrative of a major issue, and that issue is a likely prospect for a discussion question on the test. It is to the student's advantage to write the lecture notes in the order of the professor's narrative because that narrative includes all the facts and the significance that the professor expects to see on the student's test answer. After writing the lecture notes on a major issue, the student should then organize and study the facts and significance of that issue before the test.

Every discussion question on a history test includes the historical context of the issue. As mentioned before, this is the who, what, where, when, and why. The basic facts of the issue include the important persons, dates, and other facts. These details are important because if they are not on a multiple-choice test question, then the student should insert them as examples in an answer to a discussion question. Finally, the discussion answer should include the most important fact, or the significance of the issue. By organizing all of the major issues in the professor's lectures with facts from the textbook and the lecture, and then including the significance, the student can study and prepare an answer before the test. For assurance that the issue is on the test, the student may be able to discuss it with the teaching assistant or with the professor a few days before the test. A generic format for discussion of the context, the facts, and the significance on a major issue is as follows:

Jacksonian Democracy

CONTEXT: The period following the election of Andrew Jackson as president in 1828, which allowed ordinary people became involved in politics and gave birth of a new era of mass democracy.

Facts

Jackson's Character

- portrayed as a man of the people (ex: military hero, Indian fighter, no "formal" education)
- won election of 1828 based on his personality and image

Elections

- larger percent voted
- elective positions instead of appointive government positions
- most states used popular vote to select presidential electors

Parties

- started using national party conventions
- established large party structures

Jackson's Victory

- by popular vote
- massive majority in South
- stand for removal of Indians from Gulf states led to popularity
- appointed ordinary party workers through "spoils" system

Significance

- made local and national politics more democratic
- made major financial blunders in management of banking

- risked major war with France over $5 million Napoleon war claims
- created suspicion and distrust of privilege and corporate power

MULTIPLE-CHOICE QUESTIONS

One of the most common types of questions on a history exam is the multiple-choice question. This is usually a simple statement or question followed by a series of four or five choices, numbered or lettered, A through E. The student indicates the correct answer by marking it on the test or by marking the correct letter on a corresponding optical scanning answer sheet with a pencil. Multiple-choice questions have the advantage of providing the student with the correct fact even though it is listed randomly among incorrect facts. The correct fact may look familiar to the student who has studied it in advance.

A typical multiple-choice question has the following format:

Where did North American food cultivation originate?

A. Alaska

B. Mexico

C. California

D. Florida

In the above question, the student would mark the letter B to indicate that Mexico was the location for the origin of North American food cultivation. This is a simple one-answer question. That is, it has only one correct answer. It is the simplest and most common type of multiple-choice question on a history test. There are other types of multiple-choice questions, however, which may not only confuse the student but which may prompt the student to mark the wrong answer. The other types of questions are the "all except" question and the "all of the above" question.

The "all except" question poses a statement with several correct choices, except that one of the choices is wrong. A typical format for this type of question is as follows:

Each of the following food plants was a staple of North American Indian diets except

A. Corn

B. Beans

C. Squash

D. Green peas

In this question, the student must know all of the three correct answers in order to identify the wrong answer, green peas. Although this format offers the correct food plants in the first three choices, this may prompt the student to mark one of the correct food plants as the correct answer. The student may be tempted to quickly mark the letter A because "corn" was a correct food plant, although "green peas" is actually the correct answer. Students must use discipline in reading the "all except" question to avoid marking the wrong answer even though they easily knew the correct answer was "green peas." This is a common mistake in the "all except" format.

Perhaps the most common mistake is possible in the "all of the above" type of multiple-choice question, because students tend to quickly mark the first fact, rather than the correct answer. A typical "all of the above" type of multiple-choice question is as follows:

Which of the following explains how Hernan Cortes conquered the Aztecs?

A. Montezuma vacillated, allowing Cortes into the capital city of Tenochtitlan.

B. Spanish technology gave the Spaniards a distinct advantage in battle.

C. The Spaniards had Indian allies who helped defeat the Aztec army.

D. Smallpox ravaged the Aztecs, weakening their ability to resist the Spaniards.

E. All of the above are correct.

In the "all of the above" type of multiple-choice question, all of the choices are facts, but they are not the correct answer to the question. The correct answer to the question is that all of the above facts are correct. It is important for the student to read all of the choices before marking the answer. The best approach to answering a multiple-choice question is often to think of which of the choices is "the best" answer, because several of them may be facts, but one of the choices is not only fact, but the correct answer.

Selected Readings

The titles below provide a starting place for some of the concepts herein, and articulate traditional methods and content in teaching history.

Benjamin, Jules R. *A Student's Guide to History* (Boston: Bedford/St. Martin's, 2010).

Henschke, John A. Studies in Andragogy and Adult Education. University of Missouri-St. Louis-Extension http://www.umsl.edu/~henschkej/ (accessed May 2011).

Meyer, Richard J. and Kathryn F. Whitmore. *Reclaiming Reading: Teachers, Students, and Researchers Regaining Spaces for Thinking and Action* (New York: Routledge, 2011).

Newport, Cal. *How to Become a Straight-A Student* (New York: Random House, 2007).

Northcutt, Frances. *How to Get A's in College* (Atlanta: Hundreds of Heads Books, LLC,).

Smilkstein, Rita. *We're Born to Learn: Using the Brain's Natural Learning Process to Create Today's Curriculum* (Thousand Oaks, CA.: Corwin Press, 2003).

CPSIA information can be obtained at www.ICGtesting.com
Printed in the USA
LVOW01s1041180915

454310LV00005B/28/P